DESIGNING ORGANIZATIONS

THE FOUNDATION FOR EXCELLENCE

SECOND EDITION

PHILIP SADLER

**KOGAN
PAGE**

First published in 1991 by Mercury Books, Gold Arrow Publications
Limited, 862 Garratt Lane, London SW17 0NB

This edition published in 1994 by Kogan Page Limited

Kogan Page Limited
120 Pentonville Road
London N1 9JN

British Library Cataloguing in Publication Data

A CIP record for this book is available from the British Library.

ISBN 0 7494 1394 8

Typeset by Saxon Graphics Ltd, Derby
Printed and bound in Great Britain by Biddles Ltd, Guildford and
Kings Lynn

Contents

INTRODUCTION

It is 8.30am at London Airport. Passengers for the 10.00am British Airways flight to Paris are checking in at a number of desks, each of which is manned by a check-in clerk who has been well trained not only in the procedures to be followed but – equally important, in the eyes of the airline's chairman, Sir Colin Marshall – in customer service. The clerk is using a highly developed seat reservation and ticketing system which produces boarding passes and eliminates much traditional clerical work.

Elsewhere at the airport a Boeing 757 is being prepared for departure. This involves a number of different activities – engineering, in-flight catering, refuelling, cleaning and security. Some of these activities in turn involve close collaboration between BA staff and employees of other organizations. The passengers' baggage is moved into the aircraft by the baggage-handling crew, while the passengers move into the departure lounge and are kept in touch with departure time and gate number by the airport's information system, which is kept updated by BA staff. The flight crew are gathering for their briefing, as also are the cabin crew. At 9.30am boarding commences. A fully serviceable aircraft – cleaned, refuelled, provisioned with a wide range of food and beverages as well as newspapers, magazines, medical supplies and blankets – waits at the appropriate gate, fully manned with highly trained personnel on the flight deck and in the cabin. This is despite the fact that it is winter, there is a flu epidemic, and over 10 per cent of the airline's employees are absent sick. At precisely 10.00am the aircraft moves away from its station and the flight commences.

The front-line personnel involved in this operation come from a wide range of departments and functions. They all know what they have to do, how best to do it, when to do it and with whom to liaise. They could not do their jobs without the support of accountants, buyers, computer specialists, design teams, employee relations specialists, health and safety specialists, legal experts, office workers of all kinds, planners, public relations officers, personnel managers, safety experts, trainers and a host of others.

The effectiveness of the airline's organization is not, however, simply a matter of knowing what to do or of having been trained in the requisite skills. It also reflects the fact that its employees do their work with enthusiasm and take pride in doing it well. In particular, those who have contact with passengers are courteous and considerate as well as efficient.

Each successful on-time take-off is a small miracle. It will be repeated many more times the same day at Heathrow and at other airports in far-away countries. This can only happen because BA has developed a hugely effective organization, one which gets the job done efficiently, motivates its employees, meets or even exceeds its customers' expectations and provides its shareholders with a satisfactory return on their capital.

The Origins of Organization

One of the earliest accounts of organization design can be found in the Bible, in Exodus. Moses' father-in-law Jethro watched Moses sitting in judgement from morning to evening while the people of Israel queued patiently to present their petitions or register their complaints. He told Moses, 'The thing that thou doest is not good. Thou will surely wear away, both thou, and this people that is with thee; for this thing is too heavy for thee; thou are not able to perform it thyself alone'. Jethro then proposed that Moses should select able men to be rulers of thousands, rulers of hundreds, rulers of fifties and rulers of tens. Every great decision should still be brought to Moses, but otherwise these leaders should judge and decide the smaller affairs. Moses accepted Jethro's advice, and from that time his task of leading the tribes of Israel to the Promised Land was eased. The principle of the optimum span of control was now established and the first documented management hierarchy had been brought into existence.

For thousands of years since then, mankind has designed and developed organizations in order to make it possible to manage the activities of large numbers of people in relation to some common task. Until relatively recently, large complex organizations existed mainly in three spheres – the State, the armies and navies, and the Church. With industrialization, however, came a new type of purposeful human grouping: the industrial organization, with its new types of activity and with its very foundation resting on a newly articulated principle of organization design – the division of labour.

Adam Smith[1], writing in *The Wealth of Nations*, takes as the classic example the trade of pin making, pointing out that one skilled worker doing the whole job could perhaps make one pin per day. In a manufacturing organization, however,

> one man draws the wire, another straightens it, a third cuts it, a fourth points it, a fifth grinds it at the top for receiving the head; to make the head requires two or three distinct operations; to put it on is a peculiar business, to whiten the pins is another; it is even a trade by itself to put them into the paper; and the important business of making a pin is, in this manner, divided into about eighteen distinct operations, which, in some manufactories, are all performed by distinct hands, though in others the same man will sometimes perform two or three of them. I have seen a small manufactory of this kind where ten men only were employed... they could, when they exerted themselves, make among them about twelve pounds of pins in a day. There are in a pound upwards of four thousand pins of a middling size. Those ten persons, therefore, could make among them upwards of forty eight thousand pins in a day. Each person, therefore, making a tenth part of forty eight thousand pins might be considered as making four thousand eight hundred pins in a day. But if they had all wrought separately and independently they could certainly not each of them have made twenty, perhaps not one pin in a day.

Since Adam Smith's time, industrial and commercial organizations have developed considerably. They have grown in size – Britain's largest private employer, British Telecom, employs over 150,000 people; the US giant, General Motors, has a turnover in excess of $65,000,000,000. Functional specialization has increased enormously. Corporations have moved across national boundaries – IBM operates in over 100 countries. They have developed ranges of products or services from an initial single offering. They frequently serve quite different markets, selling their products to governments, other industrial corporations and to various categories of consumers. In sum, they have become very much more complex, and in consequence the issues and choices in organization design have increased out of all proportion.

Simultaneously the functions of government have multiplied, bringing into existence massive and complex organizations in fields such as education, health and social services. The British National Health Service employs approximately a million people and spends over £6 billion annually on procurement.

The development of these powerful instruments of purpose has made possible the living standards of the developed countries of the world. Important as specific advances in science and technology have been, it is the harnessing of technology through organization which transforms productivity and raises living standards. For economic progress to take place it is obviously important to know how to do such things as generate electricity, make cement, design and build machine tools, preserve foodstuffs or carry out calculations faster that the human brain can comprehend. Yet none of these pieces of knowledge can be exploited without organization, and the problems that must be solved in designing effective organizations are every bit as complex as those involved in designing machines. These problems have attracted the interest of some powerful intellects, working in the social rather than the natural sciences.

In the early stages of twentieth century industrial development, writers such as Max Weber, Lyndall Urwick, Elton Mayo, Chester Barnard and others explored the complex issues involved, which to a considerable extent they illuminated. In more recent years, following a more empirical approach, researchers in the business schools and universities, such as Alfred Chandler, Joan Woodward, Michel Crozier, Paul Lawrence, Jay Lorsch, Henry Mintzberg, Gareth Morgan and John Child, have attempted to engage in comparative studies of effective and less effective organizations and to arrive at valid generalizations about organization design from such comparisons. Remarkably few writers, however, have tried to distil the essence of this analysis and

research for the benefit of managers faced with making decisions about organization. This book is an attempt to fill that
gap.

It is written above all for the manager who is driven by the
strong need to build an organization of which he or she can
be justly proud – one which is simultaneously effective on
several fronts. Tom Peters[2] has used the expression 'a passion for excellence' as the title for one of his highly stimulating books. At first sight it may seem strange to link the idea
of passion with something as abstract as organization theory.
Yet there can be few tasks in life as potentially rewarding as
leading fulfilled human beings in the accomplishment of
worthwhile goals.

References

1. Smith, A (1922) *The Wealth of Nations*, Methuen, London.

2. Peters, T and Austin, N (1985) *A Passion for Excellence*,
   Macmillan, London.

1
ORGANIZATIONS AS SOCIAL ARCHITECTURE

Thus we know pretty definitely the factors that make organization. They are structure, lines of authority, responsibility, records and statistics; and *esprit de corps*, co-operation, 'team play', but when we attempt to determine the parts played by these factors, we find that their relative importance changes with purpose, conditions and material. We begin to realize that there is an art of organizing that requires knowledge of aims, processes, men and conditions as well as of the principles of organization.

Russell Robb, Lectures on Organization 1910 (privately printed)

IMAGES OF ORGANIZATION

As with so many other things, what you see when you look at an organization depends on your perspective. If you are the chairman or chief executive your perception is likely to be particularly subject to distortion. This is partly due to the same kind of blindness arising from natural pride in their children which causes parents to regard them as beautiful and endowed with superior intelligence and all the human virtues. It is partly due to sheer familiarity – you walk up the path to the front door of the headquarters building everyday and you don't notice, as a stranger would, that it is badly in need of a coat of paint. And it partly reflects the fact that however 'open' you try to make the organization, people will tend to give you the good news and shield you from the bad;

they will tidy up if they know you are coming; they are unlikely to have their feet on the desks reading newspapers if they know you are likely to walk through the office.

What are some of the other perspectives that can be important? Some are obviously to be found inside the organization – the perspectives of employees at different levels and in different parts of the organization. Knowing what their perceptions are is vitally important for top management, yet not all firms make systematic efforts to find out. One of the notable exceptions is IBM: this company regularly carries out opinion and attitude surveys among its employees and cannot envisage managing without them. The first IBM opinion survey in the UK was carried out at Greenock as long ago as 1964 and has been repeated every two years or so since then. In a part of Britain characterized by poor employee relations and strikes, IBM Greenock has developed to be one of IBM's most productive and high quality plants world-wide.

Since that time, carrying out regular employee attitude surveys has become standard practice in many of the most progressive companies and public sector organizations.

There are other important perspectives from outside or from a position on the boundary which separates the organization from its environment. Do you know how your organization is perceived by:

❑   Its customers?

❑   Customers of its competitors (ie your potential customers)?

❑   Young undergraduates in their last year of university, looking for a career?

❑   Young school-leavers in your locality?

❑   The chief planning officer of your local authority?

❑   Pressure groups concerned with such issues as equal opportunity, environmental conservation, facilities for the disabled?

❑   The local and national media?

❑   Investment analysts in the City?

❑   Investors, especially fund managers?

❑ The company's bankers?

❑ Its major suppliers of materials and components?

❑ Relevant departments of national and foreign governments?

❑ Relevant trade unions?

❑ Its main competitors?

A full assessment of the organization's strengths and weaknesses and its potential for development and growth needs to be based as far as possible on information from all relevant sources.

It is important to bear in mind how these perceptions are developed. It is also important to remember that once they have been developed, they are very difficult to change.

Some of the factors which influence perceptions of organization from the outside include:

❑ The quality, reliability and value for money of the goods or services. The reputation associated with a brand that has taken many years and huge sums of money to build.

❑ The approach, appearance, attitude of the organization's representatives – its salespersons, repair and maintenance workers, delivery van drivers, etc.

❑ The state of repair, aesthetic qualities and other characteristics of the organization's premises.

❑ The various clues observable by visitors coming to the organization (eg are there reserved parking lots for visitors? Are they closer to the building than those reserved for staff? Does top management have personally named parking lots? Is the reception area welcoming, with flowers, magazines, comfortable seating?)

❑ The state of cleanliness of the organization's vehicles and the standard of behaviour of their drivers.

❑ News reports about the organization's activities.

❑ The quality and design of the organization's stationery, printed materials and packaging.

Probably the least effective way of influencing perceptions is the organization's own deliberate attempts to do so by means of corporate (as distinct from product) advertising campaigns. A classic example of this was British Rail's 'We're getting there' campaign a few years ago, which was a mere whisper in the face of the thunder of communication provided by late, dirty, overcrowded trains, rude and untidily dressed staff, and decaying stations. Since that time the real improvements which have been made have been a much more powerful form of communication.

CHARACTERISTIC FEATURES OF ORGANIZATIONS

What do we understand by the word 'organization'? What are the features which should be taken into account when faced with the task of managing an organization?

Organizations are *social institutions*. They consist of groupings of people whose activities are directed towards the achievement of a common purpose. Those who design organizations tend to concern themselves only with those aspects of the human being which relate to his or her ability to perform an allotted task and thus contribute to the work of the organization as a whole – ie, aptitudes, skills and a range of personal attributes such as honesty, reliability, diligence, etc. Human beings, however, bring their whole selves to work. Their relationships of friendship or hostility with co-workers, their family obligations and concerns, their fears and hopes for the future are all part of organizational life.

The structure which has been designed to facilitate decision-making and the efficient execution of tasks will have other functions for those who work within it – it will act as a *career structure* for the ambitious, and as a *status system*. To change the structure will not only change working arrangements, it will change people's career prospects and their status.

The organization will have central importance in the lives of many of its members, especially those who spend the greater part of their working lives with a single organization. In consequence, they sometimes tend to see the organization as existing for their own benefit – to provide them with security, income, advancement and status – rather than to serve the public or to provide a good return on the investors' funds. Where such attitudes have developed, the process of managing organizational change is likely to prove particularly difficult.

As a member of an organization, a person does more than simply fill a job. He or she is also the incumbent of a *role*. An organizational role can be defined as a set of expectations held by others concerning the behaviour of the incumbent of a particular role in a social system.

The expectations that an organization has in respect of an employee will nearly always cover aspects of behaviour other than those purely concerned with carrying out a particular task. This, the *formal* role, may include such other matters as the rights and obligations associated with the job (for example, period of notice, whether monthly paid or hourly paid, eligibility for overtime payments), dress and deportment (for example, the requirement for men to wear dark suits and sober ties or for female staff not to wear trousers) and status.

This last aspect of the role is particularly important in relation to people's emotional responses to change. Almost without exception organizations have formal status systems which exercise a strong influence on behaviour. This system is supported by powerful processes and symbols – for instance, different places to eat, the allocation of company cars and the entitlement to secretarial assistance.

Not all aspects of a person's role are written down. Often they are simply part of the culture. New employees learn about them during induction processes and subsequently (sometimes painfully) from their co-workers.

Such aspects of organizations' roles are *informal* – they have grown up over time and have become accepted and established without any conscious decision processes having been involved. An obvious example that existed in many traditional organizations and which has only recently started to be challenged is that it is part of a secretary's role to make the tea and coffee.

When introducing change it is vitally important to be sensitive to the informal as well as the formal aspects of roles.

Starkey and McKinlay[1] describe the experience of a 25-year-old graduate joining the Ford Motor Company who was soon told by his colleagues that there were some important things he should know that were not written down. They included:

❑ Don't disagree with the boss.

❑ Look busy, even if you are not.

❑ Don't smile, let alone laugh.

❑ Get your numbers precisely right.

❑ CYA (cover your ass).

❑ Observe the dress code.

Organizations as 'Socio-technical' Systems

In practice, work in organizations is carried out by a partnership between human beings and technology. 'Technology' includes both hardware and software – the processes of production and administration which involve a combination of equipment and machinery on the one hand, and a wide range of systems and procedures on the other. Production technology, for example, involves not only the machinery involved but also the systems in use for production control and the maintenance of equipment.

Technology both influences and is influenced by the process of organization design. To change the technology almost invariably results in changes to the social system (ie, people's roles and status).

The Enduring Nature of Organization

Organizations may not survive indefinitely but they do usually survive longer than the working lives of individual members. Marks and Spencer today is clearly recognizable as the same organization that existed under that name in the 1960s, yet most of its employees were not members of the organization at that time. The company has expanded, changed in many respects, moved into new spheres of activity such as food retailing and financial services, yet it is still Marks and Spencer, as the Roman Catholic Church is still the Roman Catholic Church.

This existence independently of the people who are members is evident in another way. When one employee leaves he or she is almost always immediately replaced by another, without necessitating any change to the way the organization works. This is because in a very real sense the organization consists of a set of roles, rather than a number of human beings each with his or her idiosyncratic characteristics.

THE COMPONENTS OF ORGANIZATION

When organizational change takes place it will involve changes in any or all of the following:

❑   structure

❑   systems and procedures

❑   culture.

Figure 1.1 illustrates the interdependence of these three aspects of organization. BP uses the analogy of a three legged stool – take one leg away and the whole thing collapses.

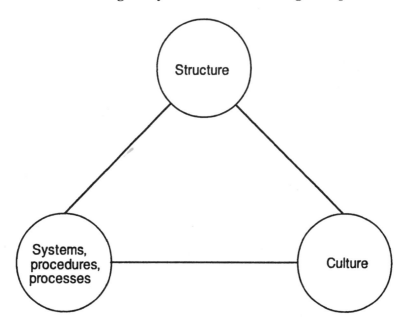

Figure 1.1 *The components of organization*

The Elements of Structure

Figure 1.2 illustrates the traditional model of the hierarchical organization, shaped like a pyramid, divided vertically into layers and horizontally into specialized functions.

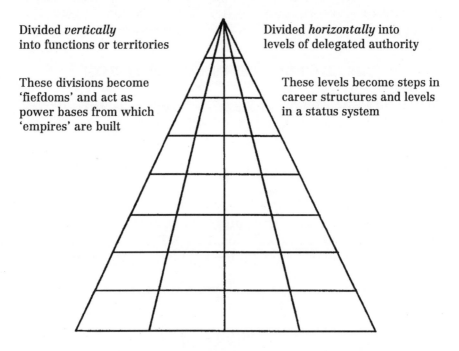

Divided *vertically* into functions or territories

These divisions become 'fiefdoms' and act as power bases from which 'empires' are built

Divided *horizontally* into levels of delegated authority

These levels become steps in career structures and levels in a status system

Figure 1.2 *The traditional model of organization*

Hierarchy

The various levels or layers in an organization's structure serve more than one purpose. In fact there may be as many as five dimensions to hierarchical structures in any one complex organization. Figure 1.3, the 'five-sided pyramid', illustrates this.

The structure for control purposes

The most usual aspect referred to when the term 'hierarchy' is used is the 'chain of command' or structure for supervision and control. This defines people's reporting relationships and

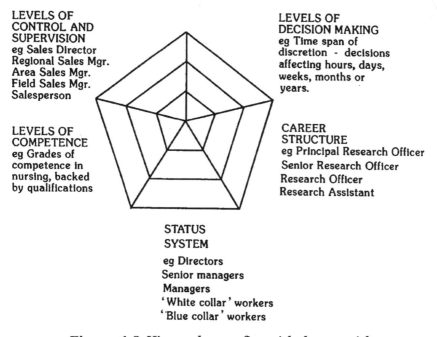

LEVELS OF
CONTROL AND
SUPERVISION
eg Sales Director
Regional Sales Mgr.
Area Sales Mgr.
Field Sales Mgr.
Salesperson

LEVELS OF
DECISION MAKING
eg Time span of
discretion - decisions
affecting hours, days,
weeks, months or
years.

LEVELS OF
COMPETENCE
eg Grades of
competence in
nursing, backed
by qualifications

CAREER
STRUCTURE
eg Principal Research Officer
Senior Research Officer
Research Officer
Research Assistant

STATUS
SYSTEM

eg Directors
Senior managers
Managers
'White collar' workers
'Blue collar' workers

Figure 1.3 *Hierarchy – a five-sided pyramid*

involves the concept of the 'span of control', ie the number of people reporting to a given position at the next level up in the hierarchy. The example given in Fig. 1.3 is typical for a large sales force. Similar structures can be found in most organization units employing large numbers of people.

The number of levels of decision-making

Elliot Jacques[2] has developed the theory of the time-span of discretion. He argues that the number of decision-making levels in organizations is a function of the time which elapses between a decision and its consequences. At the shopfloor level the outcome of a decision will be evident within days – perhaps the same day. At the level of strategic management the consequences of a decision – for example, to effect a major acquisition – may not reveal themselves for five years or even longer. For most large organizations, he suggests, this analysis indicates a requirement for five hierarchical levels. The current practice of 'delayering' – reducing the number of levels in the hierarchy, usually by removing one or more middle management layers – is in some instances an attempt to fit the structure of supervision and control to this 'natural' hierarchy of levels of decision-making.

Levels of competence/grades

In many organizations, for some categories of employee, levels of competence are clearly established and are associated with passing examinations and obtaining qualifications. In other organizations jobs are somewhat less formally arranged in a hierarchy by means of a grading system which attempts to weigh such factors as level of responsibility, skills required, etc.

A career structure

A career structure is essentially an upward path through which people can progress. In practice it may be closely linked with either the structure for supervision and control and/or the grading system. In other organizations, however, career advancement may occur as a function of some mix of length of service and assessment of performance.

A status system

There will be further close relationships between all these aspects of hierarchy and the status system of the organization. There are vast differences between organizations in the extent to which status differences are part of the formal structural arrangements. At one extreme, some organizations are characterized by several separate restaurants or canteens, separate toilets, precisely laid down entitlements to furnishing and carpets, elaborate systems governing entitlement to company cars and differential sets of benefits. In others there have been significant moves in the direction of achieving 'single status'. For example, Rover published its 'New Deal' in 1992, announcing the following changes to the existing status system:

❑ All remaining distinctions between 'staff' and 'hourly paid' status to be ended.

❑ Clocking on and off to be phased out.

❑ All personnel working within the company to wear company workwear.

❑ Single-status catering throughout.

❑ All employees to be paid by credit transfer.

❑ No employees to be laid off.

Given that a hierarchical structure includes all or most of the five dimensions outlined above, any process of structural change which has an effect on the hierarchy obviously carries a wide range of implications, potentially affecting people's reporting relationships upwards, spans of control downwards, decision-making powers, supervisory duties, job grading, career prospects and status.

Divisionalization

The traditional model of organization involves divisions based on functions – sometimes referred to as 'functional silos'. There are, however, several other ways in which structure can be internally differentiated.

Functional structures

These are of two kinds:

1. Divisions based on common skills or qualifications – as, for example, a healthcare organization differentiated into divisions or departments of doctors, nursing staff and administration staff.

2. Divisions based on a shared process, but with various skills or disciplines involved in a single process. This is common in manufacturing industry. A manufacturing division may include engineers, chemists and computer specialists. A marketing division may employ a range of disciplines from economists to salespersons, and an administrative division may include accountants, personnel specialists and lawyers.

Functional structures are common in organizations in their early stages of development but tend to come under strain when the organization grows in size and/or complexity, by extending its product range, for example, or establishing overseas subsidiaries.

The main advantage of a functional structure is, of course, the concentration of expertise. Its principal disadvantage is the problem of securing the necessary level of co-operation across functional boundaries. A high level of such collaboration is essential for effective innovation, and in consequence it is characteristic of functional organizations that they are slow to innovate.

Moving from divisions based on function to divisions based on some other criteria is a very common starting point for organizational change.

Other forms of divisionalization

The two other most common forms of divisionalization are by product/market or by territory.

Product or market divisionalization, as the term implies, involves grouping people with various qualifications or skills and who perform various functions into divisions which focus on particular products or particular markets or on particular territories or regions.

Examples of product divisionalization include the differentiation of food retailing from DIY retailing (Sainsburys), of cars from trucks (Volvo) and of insurance from banking (National Westminster).

Common examples of divisions based on markets include differentiating prescription drugs from 'over-the-counter' products, and differentiating children's hospitals from others such as geriatric care institutions. Instances where products and markets are virtually the same include British Aerospace (civil and military aircraft divisions).

Divisionalization based on territory occurs at its simplest within a country when activities are grouped by geographical region. As firms move abroad, a first step may be to separate an international division from a domestic division and subsequently to move to divisions bases on regions of the world.

The advantages and disadvantages of the various forms of divisionalization have been studied by Bartlett and Ghoshal,[3] with particular reference to international operations. They argue that the failures and disappointments of many companies in international operations are more often due to organization problems than to errors in strategy.

Functional divisionalization favours global integration of markets and manufacturing efficiency. Classic examples of unified markets which require global efficiency include transistors, radios, TVs, VCRs and quartz technology watches.

Product divisionalization favours the process of exploiting parent company know-how through worldwide diffusion of innovation along the channels created by product divisions.

Regional divisionalization favours the process of responsiveness and sensitivity to local market differences.

The Matrix Structure

Matrix organization represents an attempt to get the best of both worlds – a high level of functional expertise combined with a strong focus on a particular product, project or market segment coupled with a high level of collaboration between different divisions.

Critics of the matrix approach argue that these supposed advantages are outweighed by the lack of clear accountability and confused loyalties involved. The pros and cons of matrix structures are discussed in Chapter 6.

Structural Devices

Other structural arrangements commonly found in organizations include the following:

Project groups or task forces

These are normally interdisciplinary groups brought into being in order to carry out a specified task, on the completion of which the group is disbanded. In some situations – particularly common in the civil engineering and construction industries – virtually all work is carried out in this way and staff move from one project to another without having a permanent 'home' in the organization. In other cases individuals combine membership of a project team (for example, one focusing on the launch of a new product) with a more routine task and a role in a more or less permanent organizational grouping.

Autonomous Work Groups

These are shopfloor-level groups which, having been allocated a task, are empowered to take a wide range of decisions about working practices. They are usually held accountable for quality as well as for output and disciplinary matters. They do not normally have an appointed supervisor or foreman, although they may have an experienced and well-qualified person attached to the group who acts as a facilitator. In some instances they elect a leader from within the group.

Quality Circles

This is a structural device imported from Japan. A quality circle consists of a group of employees – usually between four and twelve in number – who voluntarily meet on a regular basis to identify, investigate and solve work-related problems, particularly those to do with quality. Quality circles are discussed more fully in Chapter 3.

Committees

In contrast to project groups or task forces, committees tend to have a longer life – they focus on issues of concern to more than one department or division of an organization but which, unlike projects, tend to be a permanent feature of an organization's life. Obvious examples of such issues include health and safety, security and management succession. Committees tend to proliferate and outlast their usefulness.

When Bob Horton initiated the large scale programme of

organizational change in BP in 1990 there were 86 standing committees in head office. These were reduced to six.

Systems, Procedures and Processes

These are the relatively formal, prescribed and standardized ways of doing things that have been developed or adopted by the organization. There will exist systems and procedures governing the core business processes, however these are defined. In Rover, for example, nine key processes were identified:

❑ product improvement

❑ new product introduction

❑ logistics

❑ sales/distribution/service

❑ manufacture

❑ maintenance

❑ business planning

❑ corporate learning

❑ management of people.

Under any one of these headings there will exist a whole range of systems and procedures. For example the manufacturing process will involve systems and/or procedures for:

❑ production scheduling and control

❑ quality control

❑ inventory control.

The process of management of people will involve such systems and/or procedures as:

❑ remuneration systems

❑ performance review and appraisal systems

❑ job grading systems

❑   procedures for recruiting and for terminating employment.

Organizational change involves both the modification of existing systems and procedures and the introduction of new ones. In recent years, for example, large numbers of organizations have introduced a system of checks on quality – usually BS 5750 – as part of a wider programme of change aimed at improving competitiveness.

Culture

Culture is notoriously difficult to define. The culture of an organization is an amalgam of shared values, a common 'mindset', characteristic behaviours ('the way we do things around here') and symbols of various kinds.

Values

Values are the things that the members of an organization collectively see as important and which consequently tend to guide their behaviour. Examples of such values are:

❑   product quality

❑   order

❑   stability

❑   customer service

❑   conformity

❑   loyalty

❑   beating the competition

❑   change

❑   openness

❑   status

❑   taking risks

❑   behaving ethically

❑   profits

❑   toughness

❑   employee welfare

❑   growth

❑   job security

❑   reputation

❑   trust

❑   flexibility

❑   respect for authority

❑   respecting the rules

Chris Argyris[4] has pointed out that there is an important difference between values which are 'espoused' (ie paid lip service to) and the deep seated values which actually do get put into practice. It is common, in the course of organization change programmes, to draw up fine-sounding lists of values. The process of embedding such values into the culture so that they actually determine behaviour is, however, much more difficult to achieve.

Mindset

A common mindset or paradigm consists of a shared set of assumptions or beliefs. For example, in the 1960s, the mindset of management in the UK car industry included the following assumption:

1. British people could be relied on to buy British cars.

2. Japanese competition need not be taken seriously since Japanese products were of notoriously poor quality.

3. Built-in obsolescence (eg cars that rusted badly within five years) was a sensible strategy since it encouraged people to change their cars.

4. The workforce was led by communists or radical socialists. The only sensible employee relations policy was one of confrontation.

Before the UK industry could begin to compete effectively with the Japanese and with the resurgent manufacturers of France, Italy and Germany, this mindset had to change. Its resilience and deep-seatedness was perhaps the single greatest obstacle to the survival of the industry.

Characteristic Behaviours

Some of the key aspects include:

❑ *Management style*   Is the decision-making autocratic or consultative? Does management practise 'management by walking about'? Are managers' doors open or closed?

❑ *Dress*   Are people expected to wear formal business clothing? Is there a company uniform, Japanese-style, which masks differences in rank or status?

❑ *Relationships*   Do people address each other formally or informally? Do they interact socially as well as at work? How much interaction takes place across different levels in the organization?

Among the many things which can act as symbols of a corporate culture are:

❑ The *image* created by corporate identity programmes – for example, BP's use of green to symbolize its concern for the environment.

❑ The impression created by the corporate office – does it dominate the city skyline, like the NatWest Tower or Shell Centre, or is it small, discreet, suburban?

Culture change is a vital element in any programme of radical or transformational organizational change. It is sufficiently complex to warrant more space being devoted to it, and the nature of culture and the process of culture change are developed further in Chapter 7.

ORGANIZATION DESIGN

Decisions about organization may reflect several different influences, including the following:

1. People's preferences – particularly those of top management.

2. The organization may be designed so as to be adapted to the strengths and weaknesses of key personnel. In such instances the structure is designed to fit the people, rather than the people being expected to adjust to a given structure.

3. Situational factors, such as the nature of the task. As Joan Woodward[5] has demonstrated, the structure appropriate to the technology of mass production differs from the structure appropriate to the technologies of batch or continuous flow production. Tasks which involve considerable risks to human safety will often call for more stringent control systems and hence different structural

arrangements for control than tasks which have no safety implications.

4. Influences due to the scale and complexity of the organization's activities. Large complex organizations need elaborate and highly sophisticated systems of organization, by comparison with small organizations engaged in a very limited range of operations. Pugh,[6] for example, showed how specialization within the marketing function increases with size of companies. Of 24 organizations employing 1000 people or less, only one had specialized public relations and advertising departments compared with 16 out of 28 organizations employing over 1000 people.

5. Specific theories about organization design which may be acquired by reading books, attending executive development programmes, hiring consultants, or imported by senior executives from organizations in which they have worked previously and in which particular features of organization design were associated with successful performance.

6. Values, beliefs, and attitudes – cultural factors, which the decision-makers tend to share. These may be derived in part from the general cultural and social environment of the business (as is conspicuously the case with Japanese industry) or inherited from the organization's own past experience. These values will affect such things as the extent to which the organization is hierarchical, the emphasis placed on status, the value placed on particular systems or procedures, and the extent to which one business function (perhaps production) is seen as being more important to the business than another (perhaps marketing). Values and beliefs are dangerous influences on organization design, since decision-makers are often unaware of the bias resulting from them. They may operate against the effective performance of tasks. For example, Thomson-McCausland and Biddle[7] have described how at the London Life Insurance Company, selling was almost a dirty word and the selling function enjoyed very low status.

Linking Organization Design and Business Strategy

Michael Porter[8] has argued that there are two basic or 'generic' competitive strategies:

1. Becoming the lowest-cost producer – offering a standard, no-frills product or service but one which, provided it can command prices close to the industry average, will provide above-average returns. To follow such a strategy requires an organization characterized by a high level of control. Examples of this strategy would include Thomson Holidays, Amstrad, MFI and Kwik-Save.

2. Differentiation – offering a product or service which, because of features which, are likely to be highly valued by customers looking for quality rather than cheapness, can command a price significantly above the industry average. To follow such a strategy calls for an organization design which emphasizes customer focus and close relationships with suppliers. Examples of this strategy include British Airways Concorde flights, Mandarin Hotels, BMW cars, designer-label clothes.

It is arguable whether these are the only possible generic strategies – for example there is a case for separating out a strategy which achieves differentiation and hence a premium price because of an outstanding track record in innovation. This is a more appropriate way of looking at the source of differentiation in such industries as advertising or pharmaceuticals than differentiation based on service or product characteristics such as quality. Such a strategy calls for an organization designed to nurture creativity and innovation.

Joe Tidd[9] points out that firms pursue different strategies at different times. In the 1970s, Western industry had to cope with intense competition from low-wage economies in Asia. In consequence they focused on cost reduction strategies. In the 1980s, the growth of competition from Japan and the growing affluence and rising expectations of consumers in the West caused a shift of emphasis to quality. In the 1990s there is a growing emphasis on innovation – on introducing new products and reducing lead times. This is partly because so many companies have now matched Japanese quality standards that quality has become an 'order-qualifying' matter, not an 'order-winning' one. This means that if a product's quality is below average, the customer doesn't even consider it. To win an order the product has to have other design features, and to continue to develop these ahead of the competition calls for continuous innovation.

Each of the generic strategies, therefore, poses different demands on the organization and, in consequence, has different implications for organization design. The three related objectives of organization design are *control, connections* and *creativity*.

❑ *Control*   Achieving a high level of control over the activities and behaviour of members of the organization. This is the primary objective of organization design in organizations in which a high level of control is vitally important if the overall goals of the organization are to be achieved. These include not only businesses which aim to achieve competitive advantage by being the lowest-cost producer, but other organizations in which control is critically important, such as coercive organizations like prisons; and organizations with operations that are highly dangerous.

❑ *Connections*   Providing effective interfaces with key aspects of the organization's environment – with customers and suppliers in particular. This objective is of primary importance for organizations which seek to achieve competitive advantage by providing superior quality of product or service, since such a strategy requires both a very strong focus on customer needs and the building of very effective relationships with suppliers. Organizations delivering services such as education or healthcare also need a very strong customer focus, to be fully effective.

❑ *Creativity*   Creating an environment in which creativity and innovation flourish. This objective is clearly the prime purpose of organization design in all organizations which have a creative task (obvious examples include advertising agencies, design groups, architectural partnerships, theatre companies, etc). Creativity is also of primary importance in business organizations which, in order to compete, need to generate a high rate of product innovation or which need to adapt to frequent and substantial changes in market conditions.

All organizations have to pay attention to the issue of how much control to exercise over the behaviour of their members; similarly, all organizations must make appropriate arrangements for connections with the environment; finally there can be few organizations that do not need a degree of creativity and innovation. Nevertheless, in most circumstances it is not too difficult to single out one of these factors as being more important, in the context of the organization's strategy, than the other two.

Whatever the primary objective, however, two further objectives will require consideration in that they will be supportive of achieving organization goals:

❑ *Commitment*   Organizations, other than purely coercive ones, can achieve very little without a degree of commitment, on the part of the membership both to the organization and to its goals. Organizations can only achieve excellence if the general level of such commitment is very high. Since commitment is very much influenced by organization design it is very important to take it into account during the design process, no matter what the primary objective may be.

❑ *Co-ordination*   Similarly, in complex organizations there is a limit to what can be achieved without co-ordination and co-operation between different parts of the overall structure. Such requirements for co-ordination cannot be left to develop spontaneously but must be taken into consideration during the design process.

Each of the five objectives will be discussed and exemplified in separate chapters of this book. How they relate to each other and to strategic choice is shown in the model in Fig 1.4.

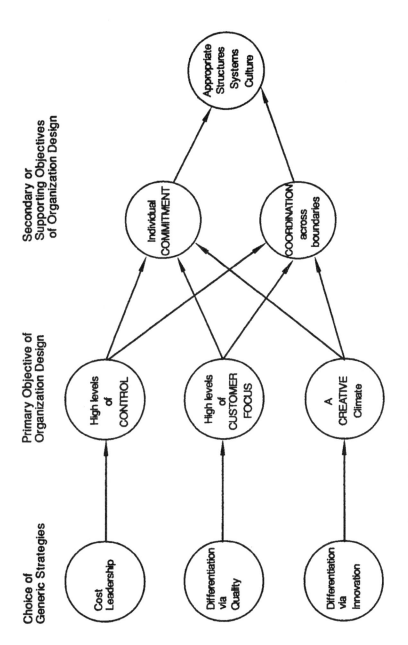

Figure 1.4 *Links between strategy and organization design*

Table 1.1 *A template for organization design*

Objectives	Structure	Systems & procedures	Cultural factors
Primary objectives			
Control	Narrow span of control Centralization of decision-making	Financial control systems Inventory control	Values: Saving the company money Observing rules and procedures
Customer focus	Market-based divisionalization	Customer surveys BS 5750	Values: The customer is king Pride in service
Creativity	Small, autonomous business units	3M's 15 per cent rule (see Chapter 4)	Values: Risk-taking Eccentricity
Secondary objectives			
Commitment	Small, autonomous work groups	Performance-related pay Employee share-ownerhsip	Values: Respect for the individual Putting people first
Co-ordination	Project groups Matrix structures	Integrated manufacturing systems	Values: Teamwork Belonging

A Template for Organization Design

Table 1.1 shows how the three 'tool-kits' of organization design – structure, systems and culture – can be combined with the three primary and two secondary objectives to form a 'template' for the organization design process. Some typical tools have been entered into the boxes, for illustrative purposes.

Organizational Effectiveness – the 'Stakeholder' Perspective

It is impossible to define organizational effectiveness without making value judgements, so instead of ducking the question of values it is better to tackle them head on, by examining the way in which different 'stakeholders' might value an organization and so be prepared to describe it as effective. Shareholders, for example, would tend to describe an organization as effective on the grounds that its consistently above-average profitability and growth resulted in an increase in the share price. Employees might take a different view and emphasize the extent to which the organization was 'a good employer' – paying good wages, providing good working conditions, scope for satisfying work and security of employment. Customers would naturally emphasize things to do with value for money, quality and reliability of goods, courtesy of service and punctuality of delivery. Suppliers would emphasize fair prices and prompt payment. Citizens of the community in which the organization is located would consider such aspects as environmental pollution, contribution to community initiatives and other aspects of 'corporate citizenship'.

Each viewpoint is valid but partial, in the sense that the ability to satisfy any one group of stakeholders is, in the medium- to long-term at least, dependent on the organization's ability to satisfy all the others. Profits depend on satisfied customers. To satisfy customers without motivated employees or satisfactory relationships with suppliers would not be easy for very long.

Organizational effectiveness, is, therefore, many-faceted. It involves not only achieving outstanding levels of performance relative to the competition, but also keeping in balance the expectations of the various groups of people involved. Marks and Spencer is an example of an effective organization in this sense, giving a strong performance in profitable growth leading to its reputation as a sound investment on the stock market; its emphasis on good human relations and pay and working conditions leads to high commitment and motivation on the part of the workforce; the customers are plainly very satisfied; and many suppliers have been rescued from bankruptcy not only by the contracts offered to them by Marks and Spencer, but also by the practical help they have been given in raising their productivity and quality.

Effectiveness in the Public Sector

To take a school as an example, the 'customers' are clearly the children and their parents. The determinants of their overall satisfaction will be complex and will include examination results, the level of sporting achievement, the 'social climate' of the school and the standard of discipline maintained, as well as other features. The employees include not only the teachers, whose level of commitment to the goals of the school will be vital, but also the administrative and catering staff. The final stakeholder is the taxpayer who will look for evidence of a satisfactory rate of return on the public expenditure involved and for indications that the materials and human resources available to the school are being used effectively. A newly appointed headmaster or headmistress seeking to build an outstandingly successful school on the foundations of one of merely average performance should be able to make use of most of the ideas in this book.

ORGANIZATIONAL CHANGE

Very few managers get the opportunity to design an organization from scratch. More often they become involved in design issues when there is a perceived need for organizational change. Sometimes this happens in response to a crisis of some kind which has led people to question whether the organization is functioning effectively, has adapted well to changing circumstances, or is in need of modification or even radical redesign. Sometimes change is of a rather different kind and reflects the need to make a major adjustment as a result of an important change or event – examples include a merger with another organization, relocation to new premises, or the introduction of radically new technology.

This book is intended to help managers facing situations such as these and to offer them useful and practical guidance in diagnosing organizational problems and making decisions about organization change and development as well as those in start-up situations.

Organizations as 'Social Architecture'

Finally, there is an important distinction to be made between organizing and building an organization. Things like the allocation of tasks, the delegation of authority, and systems for control are involved whenever the efforts of large numbers of people are co-ordinated in carrying out a common task. Organizing, in this sense, is needed in many situations which do not involve building an organization – for example, in the case of a community clearing up after a hurricane.

Building an organization, however, involves other things besides structures and methods of working. Above all, it involves binding people together with a sense of belonging and a sense of common purpose continuing over time and cementing the whole together with some shared values and ideals. It is no coincidence that so many of the world's great business corporations – IBM, Marks & Spencer, 3M, Honda, Volvo and the like have paid special attention to organization-building. For these companies the creation of a human organization aspiring to certain ideals has been a key objective. For them, organizing in the narrow sense has no significance. This book is about the lessons that can be learned from such companies: it is about building effective organizations; it is not about organizing.

SUMMARY

Modern organizations in both private and public sectors have their origins in the great state, religious and military organizations of past centuries. The management problems associated with organizational performance reflect the very considerable complexity that is created when many different disciplines and skills – using a wide range of technologies, serving a number of different market segments and operating in many different national cultures – are involved in producing a considerable range of different products and services.

The effectiveness of such organizations is inevitably judged in different ways by different groups of 'stakeholders' such as shareholders, customers, employees, suppliers and the community. Indeed, one definition of effectiveness is the ability to strike a balance between the expectations of the different stakeholder groups. This is true in the public sector as well as in the private.

In the same way, how organizations are perceived varies greatly according to one's viewpoint. The perception of the top team is likely to be particularly distorted through a mixture of pride and familiarity. Reputation is vitally important to success. It is hard won but all too easily lost.

In practice, many influences affect the design of organizations – people's preferences, their perceived strengths and weaknesses, the technology, size, the nature of the task, top management's values and beliefs and particular theories. It is generally accepted, however, that the principal determinant of decisions about design should be the organization's strategy.

The design process involves defining people's roles, which means putting them into groups, defining their relationships with co-workers, defining their rights and obligations and their status.

Organizational groupings can be based around common skills or qualifications, common processes such as manufacturing, particular products or services, particular markets or market segments, particular territorial areas or regions, or (at shopfloor level) on shiftworking.

In the design process there are three sets of tools to choose from:

❑   structural arrangements

❑   systems, procedures and processes

❑   cultural factors.

In the private sector, such different approaches to achieving competitive advantage as cost leadership, differentiation through quality or differentiation through innovation involve quite different implications for organization.

The design process involves three primary objectives which link with the organization's chosen strategy:

❑   Establishing control

❑   Making connections with the environment

❑   Encouraging creativity and innovation.

It also involves two secondary objectives:

❑   Building commitment.

❑   Achieving co-ordination and teamwork.

The need for decisions about organization is most often occasioned by a perceived need for organizational change. This can be in response either to a crisis in organizational performance or to the need to respond and adjust to a significant event such as a merger or the adoption of new technology.

This book is about the process of institution-building – the creation of organizations which are effective on many fronts over the long term and to which people take great pride in belonging.

References

1. Starkey, K and McKinlay, A (1993) *Strategy and the Human Resource*, Blackwell Business, Oxford.

2. Jacques, E (1989) *Requisite Organization*, Cason Hall, Maryland.

3. Bartlett, C and Goshal, S (1989) *Managing Across Borders*, Hutchinson Business Books, London.

4 Argyris, C (1992) *On Organizational Learning*, Blackwell Business, Oxford.

5. Woodward, J (1965) *Industrial Organization: Theory and Practice*, Oxford University Press, Oxford.

6. Pugh, D (1973) 'The Measurement of Organization Structures', in Pugh, D (ed.), *Organization Theory*, Penguin Books, Harmondsworth.

7. Thomson-McCausland, B and Biddle, D (1985) *Change, Business and Performance and Values*, Gresham College, London.

8. Porter, M (1985) *Competitive Advantage*, Free Press, New York.

9. Tidd, J (1994) 'The Link Between Manufacturing Strategy, Organization and Technology' in Storey, J (ed.), *New Wave Manufacturing Strategies*, Paul Chapman Publishing, London.

2
CONTROL

INTRODUCTION

To be in control of something means both to be in possession of the relevant information and to have the ability or power to act, to get things done. In terms of organizational life, managers need to know what is happening at shop-floor level or out in the sales territory; they also need to be able to exercise the right amount of influence on what is happening, so as to produce the desired results.

Control, therefore, has two aspects, which will be dealt with in sequence – information for control purposes and exercising control.

INFORMATION FOR CONTROL PURPOSES

This in turn has two aspects to it. First there is the need to decide what information is required for control purposes. Secondly, the implications of the information system for organization design have to be thought through. For some theorists such as March and Simon in the USA, or Britain's Stafford Beer, the management information system is the central plank of organizational design. In *Brain of the Firm,* Beer[1] argues that cybernetics (the science of control and communication) offers new insights into the problems of large complex systems such as industrial organizations and presents a study of organization and its problems based on the human nervous system. The system which provides information for control purposes is undeniably important. It is also true that in many enterprises insufficient consideration is given to it. In the last analysis, however, it is just one aspect of the overall design task and must be balanced against the demands of the other factors.

The design of the information system does, nevertheless, offer a useful starting point for the overall task of organization design since it is pointless to begin to create an information system without first having a very clear idea of the functioning of the organization as a whole and the way different activities come together in relation to the whole. Without such a model it is difficult not only to decide what key management information is required, but also to resolve many other organizational issues.

So the best starting point for organization design is the organization's purpose and the particular strategies or objectives relating to that purpose. Since control cannot be exercised in a vacuum but only in relation to established standards or goals, the first practical step is to establish such standards. Given the objective of designing an organization that is effective on a wide range of fronts, standards will need to be established under the following headings:

Standards for control purposes	*Examples*
Internal efficiencies	Profit on turnover Profit on capital employed Cash flows Levels of stocks and work in progress Productivity Quality of product
Customer satisfaction	Percentage of complaints or goods returned Average waiting time on telephone calls Percentage of deliveries on time
Employee satisfaction	Job satisfaction and organizational commitment as reflected in opinion surveys

	Labour turnover
	Sickness and absenteeism
Supplier satisfaction and satisfactoriness	Responses to surveys of suppliers' opinion
	Percentage faults and rejects of components, etc

This may seem elementary, yet how many boards of directors regularly receive information under the first heading only? If so, what makes them think they are in control of the business?

It is also important to distinguish between tactical controls which tell us how the business is performing *currently,* and *strategic* controls which tell us if the business is on course to achieve its strategic objectives. Strategic controls or 'strategic milestones' are more difficult to devise than tactical ones.

DESIGNING CONTROL SYSTEMS

Having set standards in all those areas of activity, the next step involves asking such questions as:

❑ How quickly after the events it relates to do I need to have the information?

❑ How frequently do I need to have it?

❑ In what format do I want it? Figures? Charts? Written narrative? Verbal reporting?

At this point there are some dangers to be avoided

❑ Don't confuse data (especially yards of computer print-out) with information.

❑ Don't spend time and resources recording history. Concentrate on control information which indicates the directions of change and which provides early warning signals about the future.

❑ Don't ignore the fact that some of the key information needed to run the business relates to what competitors are doing – (just as, when driving in traffic, information about what the drivers of other vehicles are doing is vital if you are going to get safely to your destination). How many boards of directors *regularly* get information about competitor activity and performance?

Where is the wisdom lost in knowledge? Where is the knowledge lost in information? Where is the information lost in data? Where are the data lost in print-outs?

Once the overall design of the control system has been delineated, it is time to consider the implications for the rest of the structure. Some of the issues which need to be faced include:

❑ Providing the information needed will have to form all or part of some people's jobs. Which jobs? To what extent should providing (and analyzing) information become a specialized activity?

❑ Recording and processing information creates and consumes paper. Since paperwork stifles other activity, how can it be kept to a minimum, consistent with getting the information you must have for control purposes?

❑ Information flows along channels of communication. In organizations such channels typically have 'valves' or 'filters' called levels in the hierarchy. What can be done to ensure that essential information arrives fast and undistorted onto the desks of the decision makers?

❑ Feedback for control purposes is needed at every level of the organization. If a guest in a hotel complains of a dirty room, it is just as important for the chambermaid to get this information as it is for the general manager to have it. How can the internal communication system be designed so as to provide adequate feedback at all levels?

❑ How can the system be designed so as to avoid giving employees the feeling that they are being spied on? (The tachometer is an ideal device for recording details of the movements of vehicles for control purposes. To long-distance lorry drivers or truckers, however, it is known as 'the spy in the cab'.)

❑   What uses can be made of information technology to streamline the management information system and enhance the quality of decision-making? For example, a computer model of the business can be developed, based on known relationships between prices and volumes and other key variables. This can then be used in a variety of ways: to generate reports, to consolidate management information from different operating divisions or subsidiary companies, or to carry out sensitivity analysis – a process which makes it possible to vary input figures, such as prices, and investigate the results of such changes on various outputs, such as sales volume and profit.

Peter Drucker[2] points out that control is essentially the ability to obtain information, and an information system provides that with greater speed and accuracy than can be achieved by traditional hierarchies with narrow spans of control. He also argues that effective information systems do not necessarily require advanced or sophisticated information technology. All that is required is a willingness to ask what information is needed, by whom, where and when. He points out that over 200 years ago, the British ruled India with 'the world's flattest organization structure' – four levels of management staffed by less than a thousand officials – many of them barely out of their teens.

EXERCISING CONTROL

The design implications of information systems for control purposes cannot in practice be divorced from the design implications of the way in which control is exercised, just as the use of information for control purposes when driving (speedometer, fuel and temperature gauges, feedback through the steering and suspension) cannot be separated from the exercise of control by means of the brakes, accelerator and steering.

   Here there are three basic questions to be answered:

1. How much control, and over what activities, will achieve the desired objectives or standards of performance?

2. How is that control to be exercised?

3. What are the implications for organization design?

Fordism – Organizing for Control

Until relatively recently the Ford Motor Company provided a clear model of a company with a system of organization designed, above all else, to achieve control. After the Second World War Henry Ford II recruited Robert McNamara and a team of whiz-kids from the business schools to bring things under control. The result was one of the most rigid control systems of all time. Starkey and McKinlay[3] relate how one Ford manager viewed the three organizations he had worked for – the Jesuits, the Navy and Ford: 'And of the three the Ford Motor Company was the most authoritarian, the most regimented, and the most driven by fear'. The company's approach to management organization until the early 1980s was characterized by functional specialization, hierarchy and tight control. The management style was confrontational rather than consultative. A famous 'Blue Book' defined the jobs and limits of authority of every employee – manual workers as well as managers. Appropriate adjectives with which to describe the Ford culture at the time were 'tough', 'macho', 'bureaucratic', 'high-pressure', 'authoritarian' and 'elitist'. It produced managers who were fanatically committed. The dominant subculture was the finance function.

The answer to the first question depends on a number of factors.

❑ Is the activity capable of being closely specified and controlled? In the case of the specific procedure to be followed by a supermarket check-out operator, the answer is clearly 'yes'. In the case of a research worker looking for a cure for AIDS, the answer is clearly 'no'. The difficult areas, however, are the shades of grey in between.

❑ What effect is close control, or the opposite, likely to have on the motivation and job satisfaction of employees? The motivation of the more educated, creative, imaginative or rebellious will be adversely affected by close and tight control. Others may welcome it.

❑ Is close control likely to result in adverse consequences by inhibiting flexibility and the ability to adjust quickly during periods of rapid change or by preventing staff from responding in a flexible way to customers' needs?

❑ Are there special requirements for close control arising out of the fact that the activities in question involve high levels of risk? Obvious examples include risks to health and safety and risks to security, risks involved in handling large sums of money.

Means of Exercising Control

There is a number of possible ways of exercising control and most organizations of any size will employ most or indeed all of these in combination.

A broad distinction can be made initially between control over *inputs* and control over *outputs,* or in other words controlling how people do their jobs on the one hand and exercising control by looking at the results they achieve, on the other. In some organizations there is a bias towards close control over detailed activities, in the belief that such an approach optimizes results. Marks and Spencer in the UK provides a clear example of this approach. The duties of a store manager are laid down precisely and in great detail and the job leaves very little scope for discretion. In other organizations the bias is in the opposite direction, with a very strong focus on results and relatively little concern with controlling the activities which relate to those results. This is very noticeable in the licensed trade and leads to the highly individualistic nature of the retail outlets – the pubs – which is in stark contrast to the uniformity of Marks and Spencer stores, for example.

Means of control which emphasize control over people's activities and behaviour include:

❏ centralization of decision making

❏ close direct supervision/narrow span of control

❏ training

❏ work study, O & M and other related techniques

❏ control systems based on recording of activities – either by people entering data or automatically (tachometers, time clocks, etc)

❏ job descriptions

❏   disciplinary codes

❏   procedural manuals.

Means of control which emphasize control over results include:

❏   inspection of finished work

❏   incentive schemes (payment by results)

❏   budgets

❏   performance management systems/management by objectives.

IMPLICATIONS FOR ORGANIZATION DESIGN

The early 'classical' writers on organization who were concerned to develop some universal principles to guide managers were almost exclusively concerned with the issue of control, neglecting other issues such as co-ordination, connections with the environment and employee motivation and commitment.

Frederick Taylor[4], for example, sought to eradicate inefficiency by increasing management control over work by breaking down complex tasks into their simple component parts, determining the most efficient way of performing each sub-task and training workers to carry out these sub-tasks in exactly the one best way. This approach combines close direct supervision with work study and training. His approach failed to take into account the effects on employee motivation and commitment of repetitive and boring work, where the contribution of the individual to the achievements of the organization as a whole is far from clear.

Lyndall F Urwick[5] formulated eight principles which he felt would, if followed, lead to the design of effective organizations. With the exception of the seventh in the list, they are all about exercising control.

1. All organizations and each part of any undertaking should be the expression of a purpose, either explicit or implied – the **principle of the objective**.

2. Formal authority and responsibility must be coterminous and coequal – the **principle of correspondence**.

3. The responsibility of higher authority for the acts of its subordinates is absolute – the **principle of responsibility**.

4. There must be a clear line of formal authority running from the top to the bottom of every organization – the **Scalar Principle**.

5. No superior can supervise directly the work of more than five or, at the most, six subordinates whose work interlocks – the **principle of the span of control**.

6. The work of every person in the organization should be confined as far as possible to the performance of a single leading function – the **principle of specialization**.

7. The final object of all organization is smooth and effective co-ordination – the **principle of co-ordination**.

8. Every position in every organization should be clearly prescribed in writing – the **principle of definition**.

An organization designed along these lines would today be described as bureaucratic. Typically it would have a very steep hierarchy, clear statements of responsibility, detailed job descriptions, and strong emphasis on functional specialization. Undoubtedly a high level of control over people's activities would be achieved, but at the expense of flexibility. Organizations like this with elaborate arrangements for exercising control have traditionally included the large banks, large retailers and military or paramilitary organizations.

The Illusion of Being in Control

Managers often feel that developments like autonomous work groups or the abandonment of some traditional supervisory practices or control mechanisms will cause them to lose control of their organizations.

In fact they are often giving up the illusion of being in control. The reality is that tight procedures and detailed reports to top management are no guarantees that employees will behave in ways which lead to cost savings or satisfied customers. Most groups of employees are quite capable of defeating quite sophisticated control systems and get a lot of their satisfaction at work from outwitting top management in this way.

There is a tendency on the part of some modern writers on organization – particularly academics who are accustomed to, and who greatly enjoy, academic freedom – to assume that structures characterized by a high degree of central control are 'bad' while those allowing more discretion and autonomy to individuals are 'good'. It is much more useful to consider the appropriateness of different systems than to place values on them. Highly centralized control systems in which the individual is left little freedom to decide his or her own actions are quite appropriate, even essential, in some situations, while systems which leave much to the judgement of the individual are appropriate in others.

It is certainly wrong to assume that people universally react adversely to close control and supervision. Indeed some of the highest levels of employee motivation and commitment are to be found in organizations like Marks and Spencer or the Brigade of Guards which are characterized by high control. Also, looking at organizations from the point of view of the customer, who wants to have to wait in a supermarket queue while the checkout operator follows her own highly individualistic but somewhat slow method of checking groceries? In such a situation we would all vote for training in the one best method. Similarly who would want to fly with an airline where pre-flight checks, if any, were left to the absolute discretion of the pilot? Exercising control by monitoring results is scarcely applicable in relation to flight safety.

CONCLUSION

For many organizations the major issue in respect of managerial control is the search for the optimum position between over-control on the one hand – leading to rigidity, costly bureaucracy and loss of motivation – and anarchy or chaos on the other. The process of making decisions about organization design is made more complex by the fact that different parts of the organization will require different levels of control.

Table 2.1 *Sources of tension in modern organizations*

	Over-control?	*Chaos, anarchy?*
Strategy	Planned, rational	Opportunistic, intuitive
Structure	Hierarchical, functional silos	Flat, networks
Communications	Vertical channels	Multiple channels
Style	Bureaucratic, impersonal	Charismatic, inspirational
Systems	Mandatory, prescriptive	Optional, discretionary
People	Conformist, convergent thinkers	Idiosyncratic, divergent thinkers
Values	'Tough minds', order, stability, efficiency	'Soft hearts', change, risk, fulfilment

SUMMARY

❑ Control has two aspects:

— The flow of information for control purposes.

— Exercising control over activities and/or outcomes.

❑ Both aspects need to be taken into account when designing the organization structure.

❑ The starting point must be the organization's strategy and the specific objectives to be achieved at the strategic and tactical levels.

❑ From these objectives, performance standards should be established in respect of such areas of activity as internal efficiency, employee relations, customer relations, and supplier relations.

❑ It will also be necessary to establish procedures for obtaining information for control purposes from sources outside the business, particularly in respect of competitor behaviour.

❑ Control mechanisms – strategic milestones – need to be

established to monitor the organization's longer term strategic development.

❑ The organization structure should provide for clear, unobstructed communication channels for the timely flow of control information.

❑ Responsibility for generating the information must be clearly allocated.

❑ The imaginative use of information technology, including building a computer model of the organization's functioning, can streamline the process and reduce unnecessary paperwork, as well as enhancing the quality of decision making.

❑ Careful judgement is called for in deciding how much control to exercise over operations, and how to achieve the desired level of control.

❑ Control may be exercised directly, over activities, or indirectly, over results.

❑ Close, direct control is appropriate in the following circumstances:

— When the work is capable of being clearly specified in terms of the one best way of doing it.

— When outputs can be precisely measured as to quantity and quality.

— When the activity involves serious risks to health and safety or risks of other kinds.

— When close control is likely to be acceptable to or even welcomed by employees.

❑ In other circumstances few controls, and only indirect ones, will be appropriate, particularly in such cases as:

— artistic or creative work

— research

— work which involves rapid responses to unexpected and/or unpredictable events. (For example, at the customer interface where a key customer need is flexibility of response).

❑ An organization designed to achieve close control over work activities will typically have the following characteristics:

— A steep hierarchy with relatively narrow spans of control.

— Authority is a function of level in the hierarchy.

— A clearly defined chain of command, with clear distinctions between line management and staff in advisory or technical roles.

— Detailed job descriptions and organization charts.

— Clearly specified performance standards covering quantity and quality of outputs.

— Specialist personnel such as work study officers concerned with work measurement and methods study.

— Explicit and strictly enforced rules covering such matters as punctuality, rest breaks, safety practices, etc.

— Procedural manuals covering all standardized operations.

❑ Organizations where close, direct control of operations is inappropriate will typically be characterized by the following features:

— Relatively flat hierarchy with wide spans of control.

— Authority located at the points in the organization where relevant knowledge and competence are to be found.

— Job content only vaguely or sketchily described.

— Normally no specialist departments concerned with work measurement or methods study.

— Relatively few rules or standard procedures laid down.

— More autonomous sub-units or divisions.

Two Final Thoughts

❑ Trust is on the whole cheaper than controls.

❑ One effective way to combine information gathering with exercising influence over people's activities is called Management by Walking About.

References

1. Beer, S (1972) *Brain of the Firm,* Allen Lane, London.

2. Drucker, P (1986) *The Frontiers of Management,* Heinemann, London.

3. Starkey, K and McKinlay, A (1993) *Strategy and the Human Resource: Ford and the Search for Competitive Advantage*, Blackwell Business, Oxford.

4. Taylor, F (1911) *The Principles of Scientific Management,* Harper & Row, New York.

5. Urwick, L F (1952) *Notes on the Theory of Organization*, American Management Association.

3
BUILDING CONNECTIONS

Industry is a customer-satisfying process, not a goods-producing process.
Theodore Levitt

INTRODUCTION

Organizations are clearly not self-contained entities. They achieve their purposes by engaging in transactions of various kinds with the outside world. They import capital from shareholders, labour from the community, and materials, equipment and services of all kinds from other organizations in the public and private sectors. In return they provide goods and services for customers and clients. These activities are continuously subject to constraints arising from the actions of other organizations with which they may have no direct links – competitors, government departments, trades unions in other industries, the press and many others. Finally, the organization is embedded in a national and international environmental context and its destiny is influenced by political, economic and social changes quite outside its control.

There are, therefore, three distinct levels of environmental interaction which need to be taken into account in the process of organization design:

1. The immediate or 'transactional' environment, which relates to inputs and outputs – primarily consisting of customers and suppliers.

2. The intermediate or 'constraining' environment which exercises strong and short- to medium-term influences on the organization – pressure groups, trades unions, planning authorities and various governmental agencies.

3. The general or 'contextual' environment, which also powerfully influences the organization's ability to achieve its objectives, but with greater emphasis on the medium to longer term, made up of a wide range of political, social, economic and technological factors.

In this chapter the focus is on designing the organization so as to make effective connections with the transactional environment – customers and suppliers.

CUSTOMER FOCUS AND QUALITY

In 1980 Americans learned that Japan's leading quality award was named after Dr W Edwards Deming, an 80-year-old American statistician. Deming and another US consultant, J M Juran, had worked with Japanese companies in the 1950s, helping them to transform their quality standards beyond all recognition. They advocated a mixture of philosophy and powerful analytical techniques – particularly statistical quality control. When US companies started using the same approaches they achieved some dramatic results. These achievements were important, but were limited in their impact on the firms' competitiveness since the focus at this stage was largely on technical improvements, and not on customers' perceptions and expectations. They were working to internal definitions of quality.

Research carried out over 18 years by the Strategic Planning Institute through the well-known PIMS project (Profit Impact of Market Strategy), involving some 3000 strategic business units in 450 firms, showed the importance of customers' perceptions of quality.[1] The research showed that when customer perception of a business's quality of product or service ranked in the top fifth for its industry the average return on investment was 32 per cent. When the quality was perceived as being in the bottom 40 per cent, the average return on investment was only 14 per cent.

Customer perception of quality showed a stronger correlation with profitability than any other variable such as market share.

Richard C. Whiteley of the Forum Group[2] points out that whereas most of the early work focused on *product* quality (what you get) most problems arise from poor *service* quality (how you get it). Forum research findings showed that 'almost 70 per cent of the identifiable reasons why customers left typical companies had nothing to do with the product'. Whiteley also makes the point that whereas most product defects are tangible and quantifiable, most service defects are less tangible, more difficult to measure. Disney Theme Parks, Honda, British Airways, Motorola, Marriott Hotels and McDonald's are, in Whiteley's view, real customer-driven organizations, since they meet or exceed customer expectations both in respect of product *and* service.

DESIGNING THE CUSTOMER-DRIVEN COMPANY

A customer-driven company, therefore, is a business which defines quality in terms of measurable customer satisfactions, rather than in terms of conforming to product specification. Companies that aim to achieve a competitive advantage through superior quality must be customer-driven if they are to be successful in achieving this goal.

Implications for Structure

Organizations which are structured primarily around markets or market segments or geographical areas are most likely to provide a good fit with the transactional environment. Organizations with product divisions may also provide a good fit in cases where there is a close match between a particular product and a particular market segment. Examples include ethical pharmaceuticals (the medical profession) and military aircraft (defence requirement agencies). When, however, products are aimed at ill-defined groups of customers, the market focus can be lost and a production orientation can develop.

Bartlett and Ghoshal[3] use Unilever as an example of an organization with a structure which is largely determined by variations in local market conditions.

In laundry detergents there is little scope for standardizing products in Europe, let alone globally. As recently as 1980, washing machine penetration ranged from less than 30 per cent of households in the UK, to over 85 per cent in Germany. In northern European countries people boiled their dirty clothes, whereas in Mediterranean countries there was still considerable attachment to hand washing them in cold water. Differences in levels of water hardness, perfume preferences, fabric mix and phosphate legislation made product differentiation between countries essential. It was also necessary to take the structure of national markets into account. In 1985, five retail chains controlled 65 per cent of the German market, while in Italy the market was highly fragmented. Different countries had different laws governing advertising and the use of various forms of sales promotion. The manufacturing operations were capable of being carried on efficiently on a relatively small scale, so that it was economic in all but the smallest countries to produce close to the market.

Unilever's structural solution – to build strong local companies, sensitive to local conditions and allowing them freedom of action with minimum interference from the centre – worked well in the circumstances. Less effective solutions were those of Kao and Procter and Gamble. Kao competed primarily on the basis of having very efficient central plants and centralized R & D. It approached the world as if it were a single undifferentiated market, in an attempt to exploit the economies associated with standard products, centralized global manufacturing and high levels of control from the centre. Procter and Gamble adopted the middle path, by developing new products in the USA and transferring them abroad, backed by a powerful expertise in marketing, with local manufacture and some degree of decentralization of control. The company ran into considerable initial difficulties, however, when it tried to introduce Tide and other successful US brands into other countries.

QUALITY CIRCLES

In manufacturing industry, shop-floor workers operate remotely from the ultimate customers for the products they make. Many Western companies, seeking to improve customer satisfaction by focusing on improvements in product quality, have adopted the structural device known as the 'quality circle', which was first developed in Japan.

A quality circle normally consists of a group of between four and 12 people, drawn from the same part of the organization, who voluntarily meet on a regular basis to identify, investigate and solve their own work-related problems – particularly ones to do with the achievement of quality standards. The solutions they develop are presented to management and, if accepted, the group will usually be involved in their implementation.

In practice there are considerable variations between organizations in the precise arrangements adopted – and in some instances even the term 'quality circle' is not used. Usually, however, three essential elements are present – a steering group of some kind which oversees the whole process, a facilitator, and properly trained circle leaders.

The steering group is sometimes chaired by the most senior line manager on site, but in other cases by a worker's representative, the personnel manager or a trade union officer. Its membership will normally include line managers, shop-floor workers, quality specialists and trade union officers where appropriate.

The facilitator – and in the large companies this is often a full-time job – links the steering committee to the actual circles on an ongoing basis. He or she needs strongly developed communications, counselling and training skills. The facilitator acts as coach to the circle leaders and groups, attends meetings, provides training, gives support and ensures that the momentum of the programme is maintained.

The circle group leader is sometimes but not always the line supervisor of the members of the group. The main thing is that he or she is adequately trained for the role.

Experience has shown that for quality circles to be fully effective, the following additional factors need to be present:

1. Commitment and support from top management must be visible and continuing.

2. Operational managers must be responsive and co-operative.

3. The preparation and training must be thorough.

4. There must be adequate recognition of successes achieved.

5. The company culture must be capable of supporting a participative approach.

6. The pre-existing climate of employee relations must be reasonably favourable.

7. All parties must be prepared to be patient and persistent and must not expect miracles overnight.

Black and Decker introduced its first quality circle in the UK in 1980 and had around 50 operating by 1985. At its Spennymoor plant in County Durham, opened in 1965, there was an established tradition of efficiency, high productivity and excellent labour relations. Quality circles built on this firm foundation and tapped the ideas and energy of the workforce in new ways. In one instance a woman employee discussed with her husband (an industrial chemist) a problem to do with the oxidization of commutators in stockrooms. Their experiments at home led to her circle's recommending an economic solution to the problem. Another circle recommended recycling worn cutting tools instead of replacing them, leading to considerable cost savings.

Quality circles played a part in the dramatic improvements in quality of service and business performance at British Airways. Here the groups are called 'Customer first teams'. The group leaders are invited to sit in on regular management workshops in order to ensure a good flow of two-way communication. Examples of the achievements of British Airways' teams include improved arrangements for tracing and delivering lost baggage, improved presentation of flight information to passengers, and better ways of dealing with unaccompanied children.

At Eaton Limited, the UK subsidiary of the Eaton Corporation, the term 'problem-solving groups' is used. These were set up in 1980. One project led to savings running well into six figures annually. The starting point was the frustration of one group member whose work area was cluttered with parts awaiting recovery. These were rejects resulting from occasional difficulty in fitting a threaded plug into the end of a shaft. The eventual solution, which involved a change in materials, resulted in less waste and a better production process. The new methods were adopted elsewhere in the group.

Although it is natural to look for examples of cost savings or measurable improvements in quality consequent upon the introduction of quality circles, many companies with some years' experience in using them stress that the more important gain is the overall change in organizational climate – a new spirit of co-operation between management and workforce. For example, running quality circles at Josiah Wedgwood & Son Ltd cost over £100,000 a year. Although clearly identifiable cost savings amount to a greater sum, the company's quality circle facilitator believes the real benefit to lie in the change in people's enthusiasm and attitude towards their work.

When quality circles fail to produce results, according to Tom Peters[4], it is for some of the following reasons:

❏ Inadequate training and preparation for all concerned.

❏ Lack of sufficiently powerful incentives.

❏ Lack of communication and top management support.

❏ Failure to implement sensible recommendations.

❏ Failure to monitor and feed back results.

❏ Trying to move too fast – instant miracles.

For quality circles to be fully effective in influencing quality as perceived by the customer, it is important to expose circle members to feedback from the customer. Where the customer is another industrial organization, arranging for circle members to visit customer premises is an increasingly common practice. In cases in which the product is distributed to individual consumers, it is important that consumer survey data are fed back at shop-floor level.

EMPOWERMENT

In service organizations people at levels equivalent to the shop-floor in manufacturing industry have direct contact with customers. By their actions and attitudes they can have a very considerable influence on levels of customer satisfaction. At the same time they frequently do *not* have the power to provide a flexible response to customers' needs. Empowerment is the process of transferring such power from management (who are often remote from the customer) to operatives so that they can use it to further the interests of the organization and increase customer satisfaction levels. It is about putting authority and responsibility in the hands of people who need these things in order to do their jobs. It involves answering the question, 'What is the nearest point to the customer at which this decision can effectively be made?'

Empowering people at the operating level inevitably involves related changes in the roles of managers. They become less concerned with taking decisions on issues passed up to them from below, and more with developing their subordinates' ability to take such decisions soundly and to exercise good judgement. They become coaches and mentors, rather than supervisors and controllers.

Clutterbuck and others[5] have usefully summarized the experience of companies that have taken steps to empower their employees. Among the most important lessons to be gained from this experience were the following:

❑ People do not necessarily welcome empowerment. They may be frightened of the responsibility implied, or insufficiently committed to the goals of the organization.

❑ A gradual approach is best. People who have been conditioned all their working lives to doing what they are told and 'going by the book' will be naturally cautious about exercising discretion and taking initiatives.

❑ Consistency is important. If managers relinquish control they must learn to live with the consequences and resist the temptation to grab it back the first time something goes wrong.

❑   The rule book will need to be rewritten, emphasizing a very few strict rules but clearly indicating those aspects of the job which can be treated more flexibly. Employees should know where to turn for guidance and advice when they feel the need.

❑   The risks must be acceptable. For example, an over-generous response to a hotel guest's complaint may cost the company a considerable sum.

Empowerment is not a process limited to the service sector, even though its applications to customer service work are the most obvious ones. In manufacturing industry the most common example of empowerment is the power to press a button and stop the assembly line if a quality problem is detected.

SYSTEMS AND PROCEDURES

BS 5750

The systematic approach to the achievement of quality standards is exemplified by the accreditation systems sponsored by the British Standards Institute (BS 5750) and the International Standards Organization (ISO 9000).

This approach has been criticized on the grounds that achieving accreditation is a highly bureaucratic process and that it is concerned with internal definitions of quality, rather than with customer needs. In much of British manufacturing industry BS 5750 has become a necessary but not sufficient basis for being competitive, since in some sectors contracts are awarded only to those companies which have achieved certification.

SYSTEMATIC TRACKING OF CUSTOMER SATISFACTION

More and more organizations are setting up sophisticated and systematic procedures for tracking customer satisfaction levels. The two main methods are the use of questionnaires and 'on-the-spot' interviews of the kind conducted in shopping malls and airports. Both approaches share a common methodological weakness, in that response rates are relatively low. The more important weakness, however, is often the failure to act on the information that is elicited.

The Avis Customer Satisfaction Tracking System

Avis Europe operates a customer satisfaction tracking system for over 500 car rental outlets in ten countries. It samples the attitudes of around 100,000 customers annually.

Customer responses are sought by means of a mailed questionnaire which reaches the customer following the rental/billing cycle. The questionnaire asks for ratings on a five-point scale for the following aspects of the service:

❑   waiting time

❑   availability of the model requested

❑   the type of car provided

❑   its cleanliness

❑   its mechanical condition

❑   professionalism of the staff

❑   personalized service by the staff

❑   billing accuracy

Customers are also asked to rate their overall satisfaction and to indicate how likely it is that they will rent from Avis in the future.

The questionnaires are printed in the main European languages. The response rate varies between 20 per cent and 25 per cent. The system generates monthly reports to station managers, showing a customer satisfaction index (a score out of a possible 100 points) and responses on each of the eight items above. Each station manager is able to see their current month's performance compared with the average performance for their district and their country. They are also given 3-month and 12-month averages, so that they can see the trend.

Customer satisfaction performance measured in this way carries equal importance with sales revenue and profit performance in determining incentive payments to station managers.

QUALITY AWARDS

A systematic approach to quality improvement which does give considerable weight to measures of customer satisfaction is the 'quality prize' approach, the two main examples of which are the American government's Baldrige Award and the European Quality Award. Both schemes award 300 out of a total of 1000 points to customer satisfaction. The first European award, in 1992, was for Rank Xerox.

BENCHMARKING

Rank Xerox's parent company, the Xerox corporation, was the first Western company to employ competitive or 'best practice' benchmarking systematically, having adopted the procedure from their Japanese subsidiary, Fuji-Xerox.

The aim of benchmarking is to identify best practice in the areas of the business which are 'critical success factors' in terms of providing customer satisfaction. The comparisons involved in benchmarking studies may be with competitors' practices, the practices of companies in other sectors, or with both.

Clutterbuck and others[5] describe the approach used in Elida Gibbs, a Unilever subsidiary. This company which produces and markets toiletries and other personal goods embarked on a two- to three-year study of product development process in fast moving consumer goods (FMCG) industries. Initially it compared its processes with those of other Unilever companies. It then carried out studies of world class examples both in non-competing FMCG companies and in businesses in other sectors. The study leads on to the implementation of what has been learned about best practice. It involves very close collaboration with a number of other companies, each of which has full access to the findings.

The process breaks down into the following stages:

1. Deciding what process to benchmark. This involves determining what the critical success factors are that create and maintain customer satisfaction.

2. Developing accurate, objective descriptions of the existing processes affecting the critical success factors.

3. Deciding what to measure and how to measure it.

4. Choosing companies against which to benchmark.

5. Measuring the 'competitive gap' – the measured difference between the current internal process's effectiveness and the effectiveness of the best practice identified elsewhere.

6. Implementation of the findings so as to close the gap.

CREATING A 'CUSTOMER FIRST' CULTURE

George Binney, writing in the Ashridge journal *Directions*[6] argues that quality assurance standards such as BS 5750 or its international equivalent ISO 9000 are not the ideal starting point for organizations seeking to transform the quality of their products and/or service. While accepting that standards have an important contribution to make, he asserts that they are only one element in a much larger picture. He points out that the European Quality Award and the US Baldrige Award allow only 14 per cent of marks for quality assurance systems. The key aspects in Binney's view are the ones not dealt with by such procedures – these are leadership, people involvement, customer delight, continuous improvement and business results. Quality assurance standards do not necessarily mean the company is doing the right things for its customers. They simply show that a quality assurance scheme has been set up. Whether or not it covers the things that really matter to the customer is another matter.

Binney also holds that the best standards are not ones derived from complex procedures but the ones which teams of workers develop for themselves and over which they have a sense of ownership.

The lesson from research carried out by Ashridge was that

every organization needed to develop its own route to quality. The companies that were most successful shared four characteristics:

1. *Forthright, listening leadership* Leadership which is assertive about standards and objectives, making it clear that quality is non-negotiable and that customer service really is top management's number one priority. At the same time the leadership actively listens to employees' views and acts on their ideas and suggestions.

2. *Provoking, not imposing change* Successful companies get people at all levels involved at a very early stage.

3. *Integrating quality into the fabric of the business* Quality becomes everyone's responsibility, not something confined to a particular team or department. Structures and processes are designed to support the focus on customers, as do appraisal systems and such things as selection criteria for new recruits.

4. *Learning by doing* Successful companies allow time and space for experimentation and learning. Feedback is encouraged and people can try out ideas or take risks without fear of blame and punishment.

Creating a Customer-Focused Culture in British Airways

When Colin Marshall was appointed chief executive of British Airways he was resolved to transform its standards of customer service quality and to make it 'The world's favourite airline'. He well understood that this could not be achieved simply by making structural changes or introducing new systems and procedures. He saw the core of the problem as being to persuade people that their efforts cannot just be focused on function or process, but that the issue of overriding importance is that of customer need. He also saw that this change of approach required a change in people's underlying values – in effect, a change in the culture. He understood, too, that the 'quick fix' approach just wouldn't work:

'To get real culture change one has to take the time, the effort and the overriding concern to get at the values involved. . . The reason so many companies seem to achieve a useful change in culture and then slowly disintegrate over the passage of even short spans of time is that one suspects they confuse the appearance of culture change, the presence of the symbols, with the needed solid change in values and their acceptance'.

(Sir Colin Marshall, Royal Society of Arts, Comino Lecture, June 1990)

CONNECTING WITH SUPPLIERS

Until relatively recently, purchasing officers generally took an antagonistic and 'arm's length' approach to suppliers. Paul Matthyssens and Christophe van den Bulte[7] describe how British and US car manufacturers used approaches characteristic of tough negotiators in order to achieve minimal cost per unit for components. They played different suppliers off against each other, offering only short-term contracts. They used their buying power in many other ways to provoke intense competition among suppliers.

This 'antagonistic' model had some serious disadvantages. First, with squeezed margins and no secure contracts, the suppliers could neither afford nor were they prepared to invest in new technology or new products. Secondly, the savings achieved by the purchasing companies represented only short-term benefits. Also, the increased requirements for product quality and reliability could not be met without co-operation on the part of suppliers. Finally, working with a changing number of different suppliers led to problems ranging from administrative complexity to inconsistencies in standards.

At the same time new ideas, largely derived from Japan, about inventory management and quality assurance suggested the desirability of a collaborative approach. The Just-in-Time concept is essentially about how to ensure that work in progress moves smoothly through the production process and that waste (of time, money, space, materials, etc) is eliminated. Achieving the ideal flow involves the following sets of actions:

❑ Quality assurance (ideally zero defects) in respect of bought-in materials and components.

❑ Rationalization of the production system via improved layout, better machine utilization, automation, design for manufacturing, etc.

❑ Precise scheduling of the inflow of goods.

❑ Committed and competent employees.

To achieve all these things involves such collaborative activities as joint training, joint design engineering, joint planning and scheduling. These in turn require longer-term relationships and dealing with a single supplier or very few.

Matthyssens and van den Bulte have provided a useful review of the literature on this topic and quote several illustrative examples. One is ASEA-Brown Boveri, which distributes a brochure to its suppliers – 'ABB and our suppliers – expectations of the relationship'. This sets out the aim of developing a competitive advantage by means of 'long-term cost reduction opportunities of mutual benefit to the supplier, ABB and ABB's customers'. ABB's expectations are listed as 'error-free quality and delivery, compressed cycle times, a reasonable price, innovative engineering capability and a portion of total cost improvements'. In return, suppliers can expect a long term relationship and a share in the financial rewards.

Such developments have considerable implications for the purchasing function in the organization structure. The role of buyer as tough negotiator is superseded by the role of supply strategist. The strategic approach to supply involves being proactive, contacting potential suppliers, developing their competence, involving them in a strategic alliance. It is a vital part of the organization's overall approach to quality and customer service. It follows that the function needs to be positioned closer to the source of strategic decision-making – in other words, it requires representation at board level.

An outstanding example of the long term view is the approach taken by Marks and Spencer in the UK towards its suppliers. The company acts as a guarantor, banker, efficiency consultant and trainer in respect of its key suppliers and binds them to it in a very close relationship which nevertheless falls short of acquisition.

Marks and Spencer has been described as a manufacturer without factories working with manufacturers who are retailers without stores. The company analyses the requirements of its customers, and transmits them rapidly to its suppliers. It employs large numbers of technical advisers who help suppliers improve productivity and raise quality. It exercises the strictest quality control and also specifies and controls not only the raw materials used but also the packaging.

Marks and Spencer's suppliers were largely shielded from the effects of the major recession in the early 1980s. Whereas 26,000 jobs were lost in the clothing industry in 1981, and 28 plants closed in the first half of 1982, Marks and Spencer's suppliers such as the Leicester knitwear firm Corah and the suit manufacturers Dewhirst and Freddie Miller all flourished. Corah supplied 60 per cent of its output to M & S and the other companies 90 per cent.

Jordan Lewis[8] points out that in the typical manufacturing business suppliers get 50 per cent or more of the revenue. Also, the R & D that goes into purchased components can contribute as much to a firm's technological development as its own R & D. Getting the best out of suppliers is, therefore, vitally important. To do so often involves giving them help in various ways. Lewis quotes IBM, Bosch and Nippon Telephone and Telegraph as examples of progressive purchasing policies. By contrast he cites the US semi-conductor industry as an example of what happens when buyers take a narrow, short-term view of their self-interest. All the companies producing 'chips' rely on suppliers of wafers, other materials and specialized equipment. In the US these suppliers have not kept up with their Japanese competitors in such things as quality and reliability. As a result, the American companies have been turning to Japanese suppliers, which has accelerated the decline of the US ones. The long-term consequences are evident – not only will US semi-conductor manufacturers become dangerously dependent upon Japanese suppliers, Japanese semi-conductor firms will increasingly have access first to the latest technology, enabling them to produce more advanced chips than their US competitors. 'Treating key suppliers as partners means being concerned for their continued welfare. If suppliers' costs must decline more than they can achieve alone, help improve their productivity rather than erode their profits'.

VALUE CHAIN ANALYSIS AND BUSINESS PROCESS RE- ENGINEERING – LINKING SUPPLIERS THROUGH TO CUSTOMERS

The idea of the value chain and its use as a management tool has been developed by Michael Porter.[9] The concept is based on the premise that any business operation exists to provide one or more products or services that are of value to others. This is as true for a division or department of a firm as it is for the firm as a whole. All have 'customers' whom they serve, whether these are internal or external. The value chain consists of stages which are the clusters of actions that transform inputs into outputs. For example, in the case of a retailer the stages might be:

1. select location

2. acquire premises

3. 'shopfit' premises

4. acquire stock

5. manage inventory

6. merchandise stock

7. provide service to customers.

Within the value chain there are three components:

1. *Vital actions* The things that *must* be done well.

2. *Vital objects* The things that need to be known and understood. These include tangible things, such as properties of raw materials and intangibles, such as market segments. The vital objects are the focal points of the vital actions.

3. *Natural interrelationships* The linkages between the vital actions, as when one process cannot commence until another is complete.

O'Sullivan and Geringer[10] suggest a four-step approach to defining the value chain of a particular enterprise:

1. *Context Analysis* This involves building as complete a picture as possible of the environment in which the enterprise is operating, the customer needs it is endeavouring to meet, the objectives of the business, its approach to competition and the nature of its products and services.

2. *Action analysis* The first step is to identify those actions which are 'mission critical' – the ones which really make a difference from the customer viewpoint. Next, the fundamental constraints are explored. For example, lack of available land may rule out any possibility of creating additional manufacturing capacity on a given site. Thirdly, the derivative actions are identified. These are actions needed to support the mission-critical actions.

Finally, the business knowledge needed by each vital action should also be identified.

3. *Linkage Analysis*   This involves defining the vital objects of the business and specifying how each vital action makes use of each vital object. It shows up the natural linkages and necessary sequences of actions.

4. *Stage Definition*   Having established what the vital actions are and the sequence in which they need to be performed, the actions can now be grouped into clusters on the basis of commonality of purpose. These clusters represent the stages of the value chain, regardless of considerations arising from the existing organization structure.

Business Process Re-engineering

The carrying out of a value chain analysis of this kind is a prerequisite for embarking upon a programme of business process re-engineering (BPR). BPR involves a fundamental examination and redesign of the processes of a business, with particular emphasis on those which are cross- functional in nature and which have an impact on the business's competitiveness, including its ability to deliver customer satisfaction. The difference between BPR and traditional practice in the field of industrial engineering, it is claimed, goes deeper than the mere invention of new jargon. Compared with practices like work study or organization and methods, BPR involves questioning the rationale for the existence of a process as distinct from accepting its necessity and seeking improvements. BPR focuses on processes which follow the value chain across internal boundaries of the organization, whereas traditional approaches tended to be carried on within functional areas. BPR is concerned with the strategic impact of processes, rather than with achieving marginal increments in productivity.

CREATING THE CUSTOMER-DRIVEN COMPANY -
THE CASE OF XEROX

In 1959 Xerox launched the world's first plain paper copier. From 1960 to the mid-1970s the company enjoyed phenomenal growth. Competition was virtually non-existent, due to patent protection, and Xerox was the fastest US company ever to reach $1 billion turnover.

In 1976 the Japanese entered the market for the first time. By the 1980s Xerox's profits lead had started to fall; the dangers were there to be seen and the decision to change was taken. Rob Walker[11] has described how the company transformed itself and became customer-driven.

The first action was to institute competitor benchmarking. Xerox looked at how its competitors developed their products, how much they cost to make, how they marketed and sold them, their distribution, arrangements for maintenance and their organizational systems. The results sent a shock wave through the company. Xerox's costs were significantly higher than those of their major competitors. It took the company twice as long as the Japanese to bring a new product to market. As an example of quality differences, Xerox was experiencing 30,000 defective parts per million, compared with the Japanese figure of less than 1000.

In 1983 a programme of change was initiated under the title 'Leadership Through Quality'. At the heart of the changes was a move away from a traditional 'command and control' organization consisting of centralized functions – sales, marketing, service, manufacturing, personnel and finance – organized on a formal hierarchical basis. In its place was developed a much more cross-functional and participative organization, where teamworking and self-managed work groups featured strongly.

To make this fundamental change work, the role of manager had to change from one of director and inspector to one of coach and facilitator.

It was judged that the best way to implement real change was by means of a full understanding of process and to use the management process as the main vehicle for the achievement of change. As an example of what was done in redesigning the management process, the number of monthly meetings for the executive team was reduced from 17 to four.

Company objectives were redefined in terms of four key priorities:

1. customer satisfaction

2. employee satisfaction

3. return on assets

4. market share.

A new strategy for the achievement of these objectives was based on six principles, as follows:

1. Customers define our business.

2. Success depends on the involvement and empowerment of highly trained people.

3. Line management is responsible for quality.

4. Management provides clear direction and objectives.

5. Strategic quality challenges are identified and met.

6. Business is managed and improved by using facts.

Another development was the 'empowerment' strategy – devolving responsibility and accountability to the employees closest to the customer. A spin-off from this was a reduction in the number of layers of management.

Business process re-engineering was used to redesign all the core business processes. Another aspect of business process re-engineering was to achieve the integration of the use of statistical analysis, as proposed by Deming and others, into all stages of the process.

The changes at Xerox can be summed up as follows:

Structural change

From a functional, hierarchical structure to cross-functional teamworking with autonomous group working.

Process change

❏ Processes were streamlined using business process re-engineering.

❏ Management processes moved from direction and inspection to coaching and facilitation.

❏ Rigorous statistical analysis was introduced.

Cultural Change

❏ The main emphasis was on achieving a strong customer focus.

❏ Another important element was moving away from a culture in which decisions had been taken on the basis of subjective opinion, to one in which decisions were based on statistical evidence and analysis of the facts.

❏ The starting point was the creation of a climate receptive to change, by carrying out competitor benchmarking.

SUMMARY

Organizations which seek to differentiate their products or services in respect of quality have to pay particular attention to aspects of organization design which ensure closeness to the customer and which reach back into the supply chain.

Early definitions of quality were internally biased, focusing on technical specification and product characteristics. More recently, the focus has shifted to customer perceptions of quality and to definitions of quality which cover service standards as well as product features.

Structure

Organizations which are divisionalized on the basis of markets or products are more likely to be customer-focused then those which are divisionalized on the basis of function.

At the operative level, many companies have used quality circles as a means of focusing employees' attention and energy on quality issues. In many cases, however, these new structures have not been supported by related changes to the structure, systems and procedures and culture. Ford, for example, tried to introduce quality circles into its UK plants in 1979 but failed completely because related changes to the management structure and processes and to the company's culture were not carried out.

Another structural initiative is empowerment, the process of transferring authority and responsibility from higher levels to those points in the organization where the ability to act and take decisions is needed if customers' needs are to be met.

Systems and Procedures

Four systematic approaches to ensuring customer satisfaction are described:

- ❑ accreditation systems such as BS 5750
- ❑ systematic tracking of customer satisfaction
- ❑ quality award schemes
- ❑ benchmarking.

Culture

Research findings show how important it is to create a customer-focused culture if other initiatives are to succeed.

Connecting with Suppliers

Co-operation with suppliers and the building of partnerships based on mutual interest are replacing traditional, adversarial types of relationship.

Value Chain Analysis and Business Process Re-engineering

Processes which involve examination and improvement of the whole chain of processes from the purchase of supplies (inwards logistics) to the creation of value for the customer include value chain analysis and business process re-engineering.

References

1. Buzzell, R D and Gale, B T (1987) *The PIMS Principles*, Free Press, New York.

2. Whiteley, R C (1991) *The Customer Driven Company*, Business Books, London.

3. Bartlett, C A and Ghoshal, S (1989) *Managing Across Borders*, Hutchinson Business Books, London.

4. Peters, T (1987) *Thriving on Chaos*, Macmillan, Basingstoke.

5. Clutterbuck, D, Clark, G and Armistead, C (1993) *Inspired Customer Service*, Kogan Page 1993

6. Binney, G 'Rising Above the Bureaucracy of Quality' *Directions : The Ashridge Journal,* May 1993.

7. Matthyssens, P and van den Bulte, C, 'Getting Closer and Nicer: Partnerships in the Supply Chain', *Long Range Planning*, Vol 27 No 1, Feb. 1994.

8. Lewis, J D (1990) *Partnerships for Profit*, Collier Macmillan, London.

9. Porter, M (1985) *Competitive Advantage*, Free Press, New York.

10. O'Sullivan, L and Geringer, J M, 'Harnessing the Power of Your Value Chain', *Long Range Planning, V*ol 26 No 2, April 1993.

11. Walker, R, 'Rank Xerox – Management Revolution', *Long Range Planning*, Vol 25 No 1, Feb. 1992.

4
ORGANIZING FOR CREATIVITY AND INNOVATION

3M – AN INNOVATIVE ORGANIZATION

3M is probably the most frequently cited example of an innovative organization. Originating from a base of sandpaper and tape products, the product range today can be counted in thousands, from Post-it notes to heart-lung machines. It is a giant corporation, with over 10 billion dollars of sales, yet it is more innovative and flexible than most small businesses.

3M is an excellent example of an approach to organization design in which structure, systems and culture interact in a mutually reinforcing way to produce the desired outcomes.

Structure

In terms of structure, the emphasis is on a large number (over 40) of relatively small, autonomous product divisions. Median plant size is 115 employees; of 90 plants, only five employ over 1000 people. Organizational roles include that of 'executive champion', committed to supporting new ventures. The career structure provides separate promotion opportunities for innovators.

Systems and procedures

Among the systems and procedures in use are the following:

❑ *The 25 per cent rule*   Twenty-five per cent of sales must come from products developed within the previous five years.

❑ *The 15 per cent rule*   Personnel may spend up to 15 per cent of the working week at their own discretion, provided the activity is product-related.

❑ *Genesis grants*   These give researchers up to $50,000 to develop projects past the idea stage. A panel of technical experts and scientists awards as many as 90 each year.

❑ *Golden step awards*   For products which achieve $2 million profitable sales within three years of launch. In 1981, when Post-it notes won an award, 13 other products did too.

❑ *The 'Second Chance' System*   This allows for projects to seek funding when they have already been rejected once.

Culture

The innovative culture is long-standing and is founded on legends and heroes of the past. The freedom to fail, for example, is based on the story of Francis T Okie's idea, in 1922, of selling sandpaper as a substitute for razors. Okie, who persisted in sanding his own face (or so the legend goes) was able to champion such a crazy idea and yet keep his job. In the end he triumphed by inventing a waterproof sandpaper which became a winner for the company.

Features of the 3M culture include:

❑ Employees are trusted. Control is through peer review and feedback.

❑ Getting close to the customer.

❑ Being patient and giving new ideas and products enough time.

❑ Having respect for other people's ideas.

❑ Openness in communication.

❑ Growing their own timber – rarely recruiting from outside and never at senior level.

Other innovative companies in North America include:

❑ *Rubbomaid*   Thirty per cent of sales must come from products developed in the last five years.

❑ *Hewlett Packard* Researchers able to spend 10 per cent of time on own pet projects. 24 hour access to laboratories and equipment. Small divisions.

❑ *Dow Corning*   Forms research partnerships with customers.

❑ *Merck*   Gives researchers time and resources to pursue high risk/ high pay-off projects.

❑ *Johnson & Johnson*   Freedom to fail. Autonomous operating units.

❑ *Black & Decker* Advisory councils get new product ideas from customers.

❑ *Texas Instruments*   Any one of 40 executives able to authorize significant sums as 'seed money' to fund interesting ideas in the early stages.

Tom Peters and Nancy Austin[1] argue that we must learn to design organizations that take into account the 'irreducible sloppiness' of the innovation process.

They point out that most innovation occurs in unplanned, unpredictable ways, often in industries quite unrelated to the nature of the innovation. They quote the study by John Jewkes and others, who analyzed 58 major inventions ranging from ball-point pens to penicillin. At least 46 occurred in the 'wrong place' – in very small firms, by individuals, by people in 'outgroups' in large companies, or in large companies in the wrong industry. Examples include Kodachrome, invented by two musicians; continuous casting of steel by a watchmaker experimenting with brass casting; synthetic detergents by dye-stuff chemists.

There is overwhelming evidence that much if not most practical innovation in large companies is the result of small groups of six to 25 people supported by a product champion but frequently acting in secret or in defiance of company policy – what Peters calls a 'skunkworks'.

Examples include Ericsson's AXE digital switching system, the UNIX operating system of AT&T, even the first locomotive built by General Electric and the basic oxygen furnace by Nippon Kokan (at the time, Japan's third largest steel company).

A classic study of innovative organizations was carried out in the 1960s by Burns and Stalker[2]. Their ideas first arose when carrying out research in a textile factory. The company was prospering, but there were some odd features about it which intrigued the researchers. One aspect of the firm was that the functions of each manager and worker were clearly defined; there was a clear management hierarchy and people accepted that they should follow instructions from their superiors. Another feature of the company was that the research and development laboratory performed very poorly and was looked on with suspicion and hostility by managers in other departments.

Shortly afterwards, they found quite different circumstances in an engineering firm. Here jobs, functions and the chain of command were as confused as they had been clear in the textile business. The people felt insecure as well as confused. Yet this firm was strikingly successful.

The differences between the organizational climates at these two firms set in train some ideas which were then further developed in studies of the electronics industry. Burns and Stalker were particularly interested in the ability of these companies to innovate and to cope with change. Most of the companies were experiencing great difficulty. Their attempts to build effective research and development teams met with little success.

There appeared to the researchers to be two quite different approaches to organization. The firms which were most innovative had a system which they described as 'organismic'. The main features were: jobs were loosely defined and constantly being redefined; tasks were more likely to be performed in the light of knowledge of the firm's overall objectives; people communicated with each other *across* the organization as much as within the hierarchical structure; there was more emphasis on consultation and consensus-building than on obedience to instructions.

The firms which failed to innovate successfully were, by and large, the ones that followed more orthodox and more traditional management practice. Burns and Stalker described these as *mechanistic*. These companies placed strong emphasis on functional specialization, and people focused on their specialized tasks without great regard for overall objectives; job descriptions were very precise; most communication followed the chain of command and people's behaviour consisted mainly of following instructions or laid down procedures.

When developing the personal computer, IBM departed from a number of standard practices. The outsourcing of some key components was allowed; open as distinct from proprietary software was used; and retail outlets were used, as was an advertising campaign based on Charlie Chaplin. The whole venture was exempt from several major corporate control procedures.

INNOVATION AND STRUCTURE

Decentralization is clearly an important component in success. Johnson and Johnson's phrase is 'growing big by staying small'. IBM, Pepsico, Hewlett Packard, Raychem, Mars and Citicorp all follow the same organizational strategy. In Peters' words, for them 'the structure *is* the strategy'. The trend is towards lean corporate staffs and increasingly small operating divisions.

Another common feature of the organization structure in highly innovative firms is the close interaction and early involvement of marketing and manufacturing personnel alongside R & D staff. Hewlett Packard has adopted the principle of the 'triad' development team – design engineers, marketing and manufacturing people being full time partners in product development from early on in the design phase.

Analysis also shows that a great many – perhaps the majority – of ideas for new products originate with users. This highlights the need for strong organizational links between innovative companies and potential end-users of new products.

Venture Organizations

This approach involves setting up a semi-independent venture organization within the company. If this is designated a profit centre it can carry out commissioned R & D for operating divisions which concentrate on manufacturing and marketing existing products. The unit may also develop new products not suitable for or not acceptable to the parent company, which may be licensed or sold to other companies.

Venture organizations have the advantage that they radically separate ongoing business from research and development. This creates favourable conditions for company creativity, but causes problems when it comes to translating a new concept into a manufactured product tailored to the needs of the markets. It helps to exchange personnel between the venture organization and the operating divisions.

The 'Innovation Champion'

Simon Majaro[3] cites the case of a major UK-based international company in the FMCG field which appointed a Director of Innovation with main board status. His task was to play a pivotal role in facilitating a free flow of innovative ideas between subsidiaries in different countries, collecting and disseminating ideas and setting up mechanisms for motivating people to develop new ideas and come forward with them.

SYSTEMS AND PROCEDURES FOR STIMULATING INNOVATION

Suggestion Schemes

Majaro gives the example of a British engineering firm which developed a system known as the 'Treasure Chest'. The first stage of the process was the issuing of a little red book (based on the model of the *Thoughts of Chairman Mao*) which emphasized the importance of creativity and the role that every member of the organization could play in stimulating it. Suggestion boxes, known as Treasure Chests, were then installed in prominent positions in the company's premises. Huge charts were installed in the main plants and offices showing the number of ideas submitted each month. A screening committee, chaired by the chief executive, was set up to evaluate the ideas; its membership included shop-floor representatives. Rewards and recognition were provided for those who submitted winning ideas.

This represents a more than usually imaginative approach to the basic concept of the suggestion scheme. The underlying assumption is that there exists locked up in people's minds a whole mass of creative ideas and that all that is needed is a mechanism for encouraging people to come forward with them. Most companies which use this approach find, however, that after the first flurry of enthusiasm the number of ideas submitted rapidly dies away. Majaro suggests several reasons why suggestion schemes fail:

- ❑ *Poor promotion* The basic rules of sound marketing apply with equal force to an internal activity of this kind as they do to persuading external customers to buy a product.

- ❑ *Lack of motivation* The first requirement is that employees identify with the goals of the organization. Beyond this there should be specific rewards for winning ideas, but these rewards need not be financial. Certificates of achievement, personal letters from the chief executive or publicity in the company newspaper can be even more effective than cash sums.

- ❑ *Lack of feedback* If individuals who submit what they naturally believe to be good ideas never hear another thing, their enthusiasm will be quickly extinguished. This will also be the case if a significant period of time elapses without any tangible results.

- ❑ *Poor screening of ideas* This is a very difficult area, since the whole process is so subjective. Who, in the last analysis, is best qualified to carry out the evaluation process? Without doubt, many brilliant ideas fail to get past screening committees made up of people with inadequate imagination, courage or vision. It is difficult for members of screening panels to overcome a natural tendency to adopt a negative attitude to the ideas of others, and the well-known 'not invented here' syndrome has a very powerful effect.

Well thought out schemes will anticipate these problems and involve means of overcoming them.

Brainstorming

Many organizations make use of the procedure known as brainstorming, first developed by Alex Osborn[4] and described in his book *Applied Imagination*. Osborn first used the technique in his company in 1939. A brainstorming session is an informal group activity, specifically designed to generate useful creative ideas. There are four basic rules:

1. Judgements are barred. Ideas are not criticized or ruled out until a later stage.

2. 'Free-wheeling' is encouraged. The wilder the idea the better, since it is easier to 'tame down' than 'think up'.

3. Quantity is wanted – the bigger the list, the greater the likelihood it will contain winners.

4. Combination and improvement are to be encouraged – as well as putting their own ideas forward, participants should suggest how the ideas of others can be turned into better ideas.

Osborn's technique has stood the test of time. It is best used when the following conditions apply:

❑ The problem is specific rather than general, simple rather than complex, familiar rather than novel.

❑ The will to solve the problem is present among those responsible for its resolution.

❑ Relationships between group members are such that participants will not be inhibited or afraid of making fools of themselves.

CREATING AN INNOVATIVE CULTURE

An approach to innovation which is based on structures and systems alone is unlikely to be wholly successful. The creation of a culture or organizational climate conducive to innovation is a vital component of strategy. There are, of course, no hard and fast guidelines for the development of such a culture, but some ideas based on the experience of highly innovative organizations can be set out.

First, there are several ways in which the top management of an organization can convey how strongly they value creativity and innovation. These include sponsoring artists, bringing their work into the organization and sponsoring competitions in local schools to encourage inventiveness. Secondly, individuality and self-expression can be encouraged by such simple means as not imposing a uniform way of dressing, not insisting on standard office furnishing and offering key personnel a wide choice of company car.

Thirdly, the free flow of ideas can be greatly enhanced by de-emphasizing hierarchy, status and seniority, and by providing frequent opportunities for people from different parts of the organization to meet informally yet not purely for social purposes.

Microsoft – The Creative Culture Paradigm

Microsoft's corporate culture is a reflection of founder Bill Gates's philosophy and approach. His clothes come off-the-peg. He works extremely hard for long hours and rarely takes a holiday. When he does, they turn into 'think weeks'. His car turns into the car park at 9.00am but rarely leaves before midnight. Once home he sends memos on his home computer for the next two hours. He is extremely challenging and takes people's ideas to pieces, looking for flaws in their logic. He has borrowed some ideas from Hewlett Packard – including keeping work units small. When Gates travels he flies economy class. The culture is informal, egalitarian, task-oriented, challenging, cerebral. It is also extremely creative.

Fourthly, the value placed on creativity and innovation can be symbolized by the presentation of corporate image and 'house style' in such things as the organization's literature and stationery, the colour schemes used in its buildings, the livery of its vehicle fleet, the style used in its TV advertising, and so on.

Finally it is helpful to expose members of the organization to sources of ideas or perspectives on the world from a variety of backgrounds. To this end networks can be built, made up of philosophers, social scientists, inventors, radical thinkers, writers and others whose ideas can powerfully stimulate the thinking of those who would otherwise become locked into the particular mindset of a single organizational environment.

INNOVATION AND THE LEARNING ORGANIZATION

In recent years the term 'the learning organization' has come into use to describe the kind of organization that is capable of continuous adaptation to changing circumstances.

Organizations are capable of learning, in the sense that they can develop competencies and maintain and improve them over considerable periods of time, despite changes in key personnel and in business conditions during the period. Procter and Gamble has developed this kind of competence in marketing, Marks and Spencer has in retailing, and the Mandarin Group has in running luxury hotels.

The definition offered by Michael Beck[5] is that a learning organization is 'one which facilitates learning and personal development for all its staff whilst continually transforming itself'. This definition emphasizes the link between individual learning and organizational learning.

Bo Hedberg[6] argues convincingly that although organizational learning occurs through individuals, it would be wrong to assert that organizational learning is merely the sum of the learning by individual members. Although organizations do not have brains in the sense that human beings do, they have cognitive systems and memories. Just as individuals develop patterns of behaviour and beliefs over time, so organizations develop ideologies and ways of doing things. Members come and go and the leadership can change, but certain ideas, practices and beliefs remain stored in the organization's memory. Standard operating procedures are the organizational equivalent of individuals' behaviour patterns. Customs, symbols and traditions carry the organization's values. The culture of the firm acts as a learning resource as the organization's heritage of learning is transmitted to newly joined members through a range of formal and informal induction processes.

Organizations cannot learn except by the process of individual members acquiring knowledge and skills. The learning that individuals achieve, however, becomes transformed into organizational learning when it becomes embedded in some way in the life of the organization, so that it remains as an asset of the organization after the individual has moved elsewhere.

The definition also emphasizes the developmental and innovative or transformational role of learning. In a learning organization the process of learning involves challenging the conventional wisdom rather than receiving it uncritically. New employees may learn 'how things are done around here' but equally (because the activity is learning, not teaching or being taught) established staff learn from newcomers and top management learn from people at shop-floor level.

Another way of looking at the process that goes on inside the learning organization is that it is a cycle. The company develops its people, broadens their vision, gives them new knowledge, enhances their skills and then in turn learns from the same people how the company can be improved.

If the resultant learning is to be transferred from individuals to the organization as a whole, there must exist mechanisms which enable this to happen. The most common mechanism is to design or modify a system or procedure – a process which obviously involves the risk of building rigidity rather than flexibility into the organization. The definition reflects this danger by emphasizing that the process of transformation should be a *continuing* one. Organizational learning, therefore, is not of the kind which involves a search for absolute truths or the right answers. It is more like learning to be a better chess player in the sense that the learner is driven by a constant desire to improve, learns from mistakes, profits from feedback and knows (with the possible temporary exception of the winner of the world championship) that the time will never come when there is nothing more to be learned.

It is, therefore, important to create a culture or climate in which learning is highly valued, one which is 'open' in the sense that challenging the conventional wisdom is acceptable and one in which risk-taking is encouraged and mistakes are seen as occasions for learning.

The importance of role-modelling by top management in this context cannot be too strongly emphasized. If a learning culture is to be successfully fostered, members of the top management team, including the chief executive, must be seen to be actively involved in learning themselves. They must be prepared to find time to take part in both internal

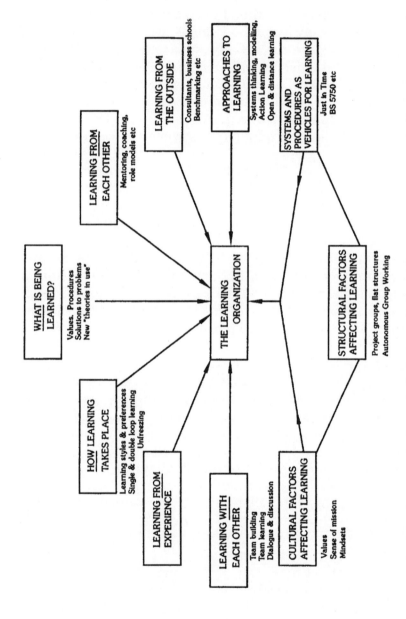

Figure 4.1 *Learning organizations – issues, processes, influences*

and external programmes as participants, to accept tutorial or mentor roles in company programmes, and above all to be seen to be receptive to new ideas, curious about the environment and questioning of the firm's most long-established and cherished practices.

Other ways in which the culture can be influenced include:

❑ Incorporating references to the role of learning in company mission statements.

❑ Creating open upward channels of communication. IBM's 'Speak Up' programme makes it possible for any members of the organization to ask any question of any member of management publicly and to get the answer publicly.

FACILITATING LEARNING

The conventional view of learning is something that takes place on training courses. Hopefully it does, but the fostering of the climate of a learning organization will involve other strategies for facilitating learning on the job and in less formal ways. Among the most commonly adopted approaches are the following:

❑ *Networking*   Making opportunities for people to interact, with a much wider network – horizontally, vertically and diagonally – than is possible in the context of normal day-to-day working. This can involve at one extreme taking whole groups of staff off-site for a 'retreat' or 'away day' lasting perhaps one or two days or – less ambitiously – hourly meetings scheduled on a monthly basis.

❑ *Feedback*   If people are to learn from experience they will need feedback in an acceptable form which will tell them how well they are doing. This is an issue to be handled in a sensitive manner, since feedback leads to learning only when it is acceptable to the recipient. IBM's approach to counselling and appraisal is a good model of the right approach.

❑ *Special assignments*   Moving people temporarily away from their work situation – for example to join project teams working on special tasks or, more adventurously, seconding people outside the organization to gain fresh experience and perspective by working in radically different environments, eg in non-profit organizations or in business organizations in other countries.

❑ *Resources and facilities for self-development*   Time off for study purposes, financial assistance with costs of education and training not directly linked to the current job, extra pay for extra qualifications, availability of open learning systems on company premises, the use of mentors or coaches and other support systems.

'Unlearning' in Organizations

'Unlearning' is more difficult to achieve than learning. It involves the ability to recognize when systems, procedures and behaviours which were in the past associated with successful organizational performance have become inappropriate and even counterproductive, and the ability to abandon these in favour of new and hitherto untried ones.

The recent history of IBM illustrates how rapidly a change in business conditions can render useless much of the accumulated experience of an organization. With the rapid development of the market for personal computers, IBM had to face the following changes:

Previously	*Now*
❑ Relatively few customers	❑ Literally millions of customers
❑ Relatively few competitors	❑ Hundreds – perhaps thousands – of competitors
❑ Predictable technology	❑ Explosive rate of technological change
❑ Foremost importance of hardware	❑ Foremost importance of systems, software and solutions
❑ Reliance on own direct sales force	❑ Marketing through business partners
❑ Standard terms of business	❑ Many ways of doing business

In adjusting to these new conditions, IBM at first encountered considerable difficulties – in the words of chief executive Akers, 'We went off track'. These difficulties reflect the enormous problems associated with 'unlearning' and abandoning practices which over many years had led to IBM's winning a reputation as the world's best-managed corporation.

STRATEGIC MANAGEMENT AS A LEARNING PROCESS – THE CASE OF MOTOROLA

A key talent for Motorola today is software expertise. Up to about ten years ago the key design skills for Motorola products were electrical engineering and mechanical engineering. Since then software solutions to design problems have become increasingly important. In setting out to recruit more software people the company discovered two things: first, that 'there were not enough software people anywhere on planet earth at that point in time, and that they were mainly being chewed up by the computer companies'. Secondly, that the expertise of writing software programs for the communications industry was mainly held captive by the Ericssons and the AT&Ts of the world.

Motorola's need for software expertise had grown to the extent that recruiting and retaining them had become designated as one of the key business issues. By this time, much had been learned about what attracted software people to a company and what motivated them.

'Good, progressive computer companies don't manage software people – they don't care what time they come in to work, because they know these people will get on a run and go for 48 to 72 hours straight writing a section of the program while it's all complete in their heads; and they don't care about going to the cafeteria; they will have food at their workstations. So there are no rules that say 'keep things neat'; software people are allowed to just come in and 'do their thing' – they may disappear for three days and then show back up and work at night etc. This flexibility is necessary to allow their creativity to work best'.

Experience has shown Motorola that when these people are brought in, what they will do is get back on the phone to their former employer and talk to four or five friends and say, 'It's a better place to work, come on over':

> What they are looking for is a lot of work motivation. Intrinsic motivation among software people is this really interesting stuff – it's designing a cellular switch program so that a city the size of Chicago can seamlessly pass off phone messages when it passes the forecast half a million users and is now at a million users – and software people think, 'Hum, there's no solution for that; hum, that sounds really exciting!' That's how you attract software people. But then if you over-manage them and restrict them, you will lose them – especially when there's a lot of very intriguing software issues out there.

The company faced the fact that it did not have much of a history or tradition with software, and that in Chicago it was badly located relative to the three main centres of software expertise in the US – around Boston, Silicon Valley, and the Raleigh, Durham 'research triangle' in North Carolina. (A fourth one of particular interest to Motorola was developing around Fort Worth, centred on Northern Telecom and Ericsson).

The retraining of surplus-to-requirements mechanical engineers had been tried, but involved huge training costs. Also, 'there's an attitude or mentality towards software work that brought software people to it when they had a choice of universities in the first place'.

This attitude, it was found, was not necessarily capable of being developed by retraining. It was a question of what gives people excitement in their work – convergent or divergent thinking mechanical engineers like to converge on a solution and sew things up before moving on. Software people like divergence – rather like playing Nintendo games – finding the next door that opens up a whole new space they can play with.

Retraining thus did not prove capable of closing the gap between the planned requirement for software people and the numbers being recruited.

In consequence, a fresh approach to the problem was adopted. When the company started to plan its senior executive training programme for 1990 it decided to focus on the software issue. The company's chairman, George Fisher, said:

It's all well and good to bring the top people in here and say: software is the issue of the future but we don't have enough people, etc, but that's not good enough. Why don't we look at something different. How can we get some people around here *owning* that issue and working it through to a solution?

The executive education programme was then redesigned on action learning lines, following the model developed by Reg Revans in which learning takes place in the context of analyzing, developing solutions and implementing change in respect of problems which are not only real ones but also ones of critical importance to the organization. The problem was redefined as how to create an environment inside Motorola such that it would attract 'best-in-class' software people and such that, once attracted to this environment, they would find that they would prosper. It was recognized that:

> The secret of hiring software people is having a cadre of very satisfied software people already working for you, because it's networked. The people who studied in software in MIT are the people who worked five years ago at DEC and know each other. They are the ones with these electronic networks in their computers; they are the ones who talk to each other in real time.

> So once Motorola employees start saying, 'great place to work, great labs, you can make your own hours, there are some incredibly challenging issues, pay is good, Chicago's a great area to live, good jazz clubs, etc, etc' – whatever it might be: that's off down the wire. Then you start getting people calling in saying, 'Do you have any software positions?' – well, 'Yes, we do'. For years up until now the phone did not ring from software people, they didn't think of Motorola as that kind of place.

It took a year to redesign the senior executive programme, so it began in 1991, not 1990. The chairman personally invited 25 top people to participate in it. In the invitation he advised the participants of the following objectives:

❑   First, to become fully informed and educated about what would be a best-in-class work environment for software people and to come up with a plan for achieving it.

❏ Secondly, to invent a process for the realization of this plan. 'You're going to recommend, we'll agree and you're going to go do it; you are the implementers'.

❏ Thirdly, to learn how to make these changes inside the corporation, to document how you made these changes and begin to leave a legacy of the new model for organizational change and inside advice – 'that's the real organization learning'.

The group is now well into this process and have set themselves a five year target for implementation. (This is the company in which, in 1979, the head of sales for the communication business worldwide stood up at a meeting and said, 'Our quality stinks'. In 1988 Motorola won the coveted Malcolm Baldrige National Quality Award).

The group has organized itself into sub-groups focused on issues. Some are to do with technical issues such as the design of workstations or the internal standards and codings in use in different parts of the company. Others are working on 'people' issues such as recruitment strategies, motivation and training to combat obsolescence.

It is, of course, too early on in this process to be able to judge its success. A significant factor, however, is the direct support and interest of the chairman, George Fisher, himself a PhD in Applied Mathematics and a former Bell Labs research scientist.

ORGANIZING FOR CREATIVITY –
THE CASE OF BELL LABS

AT&T Bell Laboratories is an extremely large R & D organization, with 19,000 employees in 16 locations. It is part of AT&T. Its approach has been described by Solomon J. Buchsbaum, Executive Vice-President.[7] The starting point is the organization's mission, which serves as the major motivation for creativity. For it to serve this purpose it must be one which *all* members of the organization – not just the top corporate managers – can associate with and take pride in – one in which everyone, but particularly scientists and engineers, can find 'personal meaning and reward.' This means that the mission has to be more than just 'making a profit' or 'maximizing return to stockholders'.

Bell Laboratories has been guided by a sense of mission since its origin in 1911 as the fundamental research group of the Western Electric Company's Engineering Department.

Until the divestiture of AT&T in 1984, the Bell Lab's mission was to provide the operating companies in the group with the technology needed to deliver a quality, low cost, universal connection service. Since 1984 the mission of the parent company has changed to one of bringing everyone the broader, more varied services of the 'information age' – and the mission of the Labs is to provide the technology AT&T needs to be a world leader in information systems and services as well as telecommunications.

Given the guidance and sense of direction provided by the mission, the additional elements in Bell's approach are:

❑ The way it is organized so as to attempt to gain the best of both worlds by combining the best features of both the centralized and decentralized approaches to structure.

The centralized aspect is that the Labs are organized along functional lines. This is because the common technologies of microelectronics, software and photonics are involved in such a high proportion of the Labs' work, as well as being the common technologies underlying some 12 billion dollars' worth of products manufactured annually by AT&T. Much hardware is produced as standard and is customized via software using common design techniques. In view of this, it is vital to share common human and technical resources, avoid duplications of effort and pool information.

The decentralized aspect exists in the focusing of design and development work on specific projects or on the needs of particular business units.

Another aspect of organization design is to organize into groups which are as small as possible and to give them as much autonomy as possible. It is the case that complex projects will in the end involve hundreds of people, but they begin with small teams and increase the team size gradually as needed.

❑ An approach to research management based on three factors known as 'the 3 Fs' – funding, focus and freedom. Funding refers to the sustained funding support needed to provide both continuity of long-term research and confidence on the part of research workers. Focus reflects a concentration of research effort on the areas determined by the mission, and freedom is the 'space' given to the individual scientist to work within a particular field of his or her choice within that broad overall mission.

As an example of the impact of focus and freedom taken together, Buchsbaum quotes the Unix operating system which was created by two researchers, Dennis M. Ritchie and Kenneth Thompson, who a decade previously had become dissatisfied with progress on a very large, ambitious and ultimately unsuccessful project, and used their freedom to pursue alternatives within the same broad framework of objectives, with outstandingly successful results.

❑ The company's strong emphasis on an open publication policy which serves several purposes including enhancing the Labs' access to other people's research, attracting top-level talent and maintaining a reputation for leading edge R & D.

❑ A highly competitive approach to searching out and hiring the brightest, most talented and most imaginative people, allied to recognition of an obligation to work with and contribute to the American education system,

> to see that the reservoir of trained talent on which we all depend does not run dry. The talent that we draw from these schools and from other institutions around the world represents our greatest asset. It also represents a variety of persons of various backgrounds, interests and personality types, whose individuality as well as talents must be recognized, respected and sometimes even tolerated.

❑ Providing a work climate that is intellectually and technically challenging – 'a problem-rich environment that fuels the spirit of inquiry'.

❑ Expecting managers of research teams to be 'more leaders than managers, allowing as much personal creativity as possible to take place in their teams...'.

❑ Supporting an extensive programme of continuing education, both through a wide-ranging programme of in-house courses and also by providing opportunities to return to the campus for advanced degrees.

CONCLUSION

Organizing for creativity and innovation and flexibility gives rise to special problems, since there are inherent contradictions between the underlying concepts of organization – such as order, predictability, routinization and standardization – and the requirements for creativity to flourish and flexibility to prevail. Creativity tends to shun the imposition of order, to seek to evade control. Moreover, it is when things are most well regulated that they are most resistant to change. Where innovation and/or the ability to adapt rapidly to changing circumstances are vital for organizational survival and success there is no alternative, however, but to 'unlearn' most of the rules about organization design which were developed during a more stable period in our history and to throw out the time-honoured procedural manuals and systems. This is never an easy thing to do and it is most difficult for very large organizations. It is noticeable that size is no longer seen as such a desirable corporate asset as in the past, and a growing tendency for companies to decentralize can be identified, even to the extent of divesting large sections of the business.

SUMMARY

Organizations which are highly creative and innovative have the following characteristics:

❑ *Structure* Decentralized with relatively small, highly autonomous business units – 'skunkworks', venture organizations and 'flat' structures.

❑ *Systems and procedures* Allowances of time for people to work on 'unofficial' projects. Specific targets for new product development. Innovative 'champions'. Special incentives and awards for innovation. Suggestion schemes. Laboratories etc open 24 hours. Brainstorming sessions.

❑ *Culture* The most common features include:

— a high level of trust

— the 'freedom to fail'

— respect for other people's ideas

— openness in communications

— minimal status differences

— links with the arts.

Most innovation occurs in unplanned, unpredictable ways, often in industries which are quite unrelated to the nature of the invention.

The concept of the 'learning organization' has developed in recent years as a means of characterizing organizations which continuously adapt to change through innovation. The creation of a learning organization involves developing a culture in which learning is highly valued. The example needs to be set by top management. Learning is facilitated by:

❑ networking

❑ providing feedback

❑ special assignments

❑ resources and time off for study

❑ facilities for individual self-development.

Unlearning – particularly for once outstandingly successful companies like IBM – is more difficult than learning.

References

1. Peters, T and Austin, N (1985) *A Passion for Excellence*, Macmillan, Basingstoke.

2. Burns, T and Stalker, G M (1961) *The Management of Innovation*, Tavistock, London.

3. Majaro, S (1988) *The Creative Gap*, Longmans, Harlow.

4. Osborn, A (1953) *Applied Imagination*, Charles Scribner & Sons, New York.

5. Beck, M, 'Learning Organizations - How to Create Them', *Industrial and Commercial Training*, Vol 21, May/June, 1989.

6. Hedberg, B (1981) 'How Organizations Learn and Unlearn' in P.C. Mystrom and W. Starbuck (eds) *Handbook of Organization Design*, Oxford University Press, Oxford.

7. Buchsbaum, S J, 'Managing for Creativity – For Fun and For Profit', *International Journal of Technology Management* Vol 1, Nos 1/2, 1986.

5
DESIGNING ORGANIZATIONS FOR EMPLOYEE COMMITMENT

INTRODUCTION

According to Roy Thornton, plant manager with Procter and Gamble, 'Americans will one day thank the Japanese for waking us up'. His plant in Greensboro, North Carolina, manufactures hair care products, dentifrice and deodorants. Its 500 employees are grouped into teams and every day each team meets for 30 minutes (in company time) in its own meeting room, to plan and co-ordinate its activities. As well as being responsible for a clearly defined business function such as manufacturing, packaging or distributing a particular brand of product, the team also allocates its members to share in plant-wide tasks such as maintenance, cleaning and even office work: 'Here there is no such thing as an accountant'. Employee involvement is not, however, restricted to the organization and execution of everyday tasks. It begins at the strategic level, focusing on how to outperform P & G's major competitors – not just the traditional ones, Colgate and Unilever, but the more recent threat from Japan in the shape of Kao. Information about strategy, tactics, profits and market share is fully disclosed. The plant's organization structure is shown in Fig. 5.1. When Roy Thornton embarked on his radical approach to the running of the factory he was not allowed to give certain information to the shopfloor, on the grounds that it might leak through to the competition. So he used his initiative and obtained the information from Nielson – the market research agency – thus demonstrating that the material was already in the public domain. This degree of openness has now been adopted company-wide. Strategic issues are debated annually when the plant is shut down and everybody goes offsite for a strategic workshop in which the corporate vice-presidents participate.

Thornton believes strongly in the importance of innovation and argues that it springs from the creativity of people of all kinds and at all levels – 'God didn't just make managers the creative ones'. He taps worker creativity in two ways – first through the work teams described above, and secondly through 'diagonal slice' groups each consisting of a cross-section of employees. These groups designed the production system and the pay system, and take decisions about manning and recruiting. Thornton accepts their decisions provided they do not violate the 'Greensboro Principles' – a set of values developed in discussion with employees and printed on a plastic card carried by every employee. The key values are:

❑ high standards of performance

❑ winning through teamwork

❑ being an owner – managing the business, through the team as if we were using our own personal resources

❑ treating each employee as an individual

❑ honesty and integrity

❑ good communication

❑ a safe, clean, healthy working environment

❑ employment stability through building a successful business.

The shared values are given further expression through a list of 'golden threads' which bind the members of the organiza-

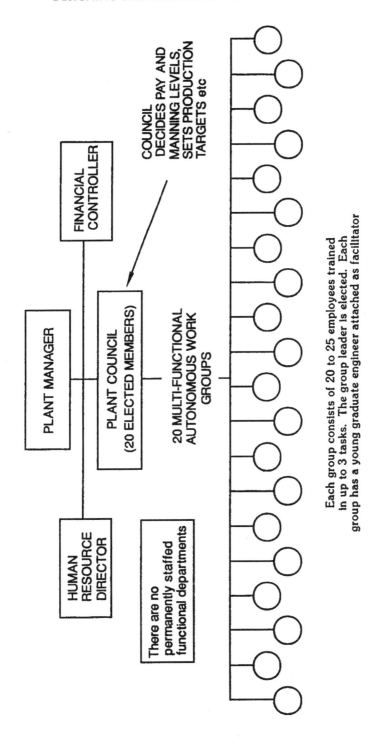

Figure 5.1 *The Greensboro Procter and Gamble plant organization*

tion together. These are printed on the reverse side of the same plastic card:

❑ safety

❑ high quality

❑ low cost

❑ customer service

❑ a multicultural organization effectively using the abilities of people of both sexes and all races

❑ timely information

❑ high appearance standards.

Most organizations are designed primarily to facilitate control of the activities of one group of people (the employees) by another group of people (the managers). Designs which have these objectives reflect a number of assumptions. The first and most obvious is that managers know best; the second is that employees are not to be trusted; the third is that controlling what people do with their hands and feet is more important than winning their hearts and minds.

Some of the most spectacularly successful organizations in the modern world have been designed on the basis of an entirely different philosophy – one based on the view that employee motivation and commitment is the most powerful competitive weapon of all. Procter and Gamble's Greensboro plant is one of a growing number of examples of organizations representing this approach.

Many of the ideas being built into radical approaches to organization design in North America and Western Europe have been modelled on or adopted from Japanese management practice – in particular such things as quality circles and an egalitarian approach to working conditions. Above all, Japanese industry's success in the sphere of product quality and the achievement of 'zero defects' has clearly demonstrated that quality and commitment are inseparable.

MOTIVATION AND THE DESIGN OF INDIVIDUAL JOBS

The level of motivation and commitment to the organization on the part of the individual worker will to a considerable extent reflect his or her satisfaction with the job itself – the actual work he or she is required to do.

Taylorism

In designing jobs, managers are usually trying to maximize productivity. The traditional approach is typified by the work of Frederick Taylor,[1] whose approach was based on the twin assumptions that workers were essentially stupid and lazy.

An engineer from Philadelphia who trained as a machinist, Taylor was appalled by the inefficiency of the industrial practices he witnessed, and set out to demonstrate how managers and workers could benefit by adopting a more 'scientific' approach. He felt that inefficiency was caused by what he called 'systematic soldiering' – the deliberate restriction of output by workers anxious to sustain their employment. Soldiering was easy because management control was weak, and because discretion over work methods was left to individual workers who wasted time and effort with inefficient work practices based on rule of thumb. Managers expected their employees to have the appropriate skills for the work they were given, or to learn what to do from those around them. Notions of systematic job specifications, clearly established responsibilities, and training needs analysis were not appreciated. Taylor sought to change that.

He argued that manual and mental work should be separated. Management, he claimed, should specialize in planning and organizing work, and workers should specialize in actually doing it. Taylor regarded this as a way of ensuring industrial harmony, as everyone would know clearly what was expected of them and what their responsibilities were. He also saw the clear advantages in making individuals specialize in activities in which they would become expert and highly proficient.

His technique for designing manual jobs involved the following steps. First, decide the optimum degree of task fragmentation, breaking down complex jobs into their simple component parts. Second, determine the most efficient way of performing each part of the work. Studies should be carried out to discover the best way of doing each of the fragmented tasks, and to design the layout of the workplace and tools to be used so that unnecessary movements could be eliminated. Finally, select and train employees to carry out the fragmented tasks in exactly the best way, and reward them for above-average performance.

Clearly, task fragmentation can have a number of advantages for the organization that adopts this approach. Individual workers do not need to be given expensive and time-consuming training, and those who leave or who prove to be unreliable can easily by replaced. Specialization in one small task makes it possible for people to work very fast at it. Less skilled work is lower-paid work. And it is easier to observe and control workers doing simple activities.

At the same time, task fragmentation gives rise to serious motivational problems. The work is repetitive and boring. The contribution of the individual to the work of the organization as a whole is comparatively meaningless. Monotony can lead to apathy, alienation and conflict.

The most frequently quoted research findings on the subject of job design and employee motivation are those of Fred Herzberg.[2] His research team asked people to describe times when they had been particularly happy or unhappy at work. When people talked of times when they had been unhappy the things they mentioned fell mainly under the following headings:

❑ company policy and administration

❑ supervision (technical)

❑ salary

❑ interpersonal relations (supervisory)

❑ working conditions.

On the other hand, when people described occasions when they were particularly happy the things they talked about were grouped as follows:

- ❑ achievement
- ❑ recognition
- ❑ the work itself
- ❑ responsibility.

The two lists are clearly different – they refer to quite different kinds of experience; they are not opposite ends of the same scale. The implication is evident. If management does things to improve working conditions, or raises salaries (what Herzberg calls 'hygiene' factors), grounds for dissatisfaction may be removed but nothing will have been done to create positive motivation. In order to raise motivation, management must pay attention to the nature of the work itself, the extent to which it gives people a sense of achievement and the ways in which people are given recognition for their achievements.

Herzberg's findings have been replicated by some researchers, but challenged by others. The most valid challenge is based on evidence that workers from different socioeconomic or educational backgrounds or in different cultural settings are motivated in different ways, indicating that human motivation is a complex matter not capable of being reduced to a simple formula.

What is important is to try to develop insight into the motivation of particular groups of workers and design the organization in which they work accordingly.

Job design experiments in Norway in the 1960s[3] resulted in a set of criteria for designing motivating jobs which is still useful today:

At the level of the individual

1. *Optimum variety* Avoiding the extremes of monotonous repetition which lead to boredom and fatigue, and too much variety which leads to inefficiency and stress.

2. *Meaningful work* A task which is a meaningful whole – a recognizable component or sub-assembly, for example, or a report which has been typed, corrected, reproduced and bound.

3. *Optimum length of work cycle*   If this is too short, too much time is spent finishing off and starting up, which is inefficient and frustrating. If it is too long, boredom and fatigue set in.

4. *Influence over quantity and quality of outputs*   Although minimum standards may have to be imposed by management, workers are more likely to try to exceed these if given the freedom to set themselves higher standards.

5. *Knowledge of results*   Reinforcing the need to achieve by providing knowledge of results.

6. *Respect*   The job should be so designed and described that it creates respect for the skill, care, service, effort, or strength of the performer.

7. *Contribution*   The contribution of the job to overall company objectives should be clear.

At the level of the group

1. *Interdependence*   Reinforce satisfying group cohesion by means of interacting tasks, ease of communication between co-workers, and physical lay-out of workstations.

2. *Mutual support*   Where tasks involve danger or some other form of stress, provide group support for individuals through such devices as strong group identity, opportunity for off-duty group activities, supportive leadership styles, etc.

3. *Relative autonomy*   The group should be given some degree of responsibility for task allocation, discipline, output norms and quality standards.

In recent years the term 'empowerment' has increasingly been used to describe a range of measures leading to greater authority, responsibility, autonomy and involvement in decisions on the part of individuals and work groups at the operational or shop-floor level.

Four well tried approaches to job design which minimize standardization, specialization and controls are known as job rotation, job enlargement, job enrichment and autonomous group working.

❑ *Job rotation* aims at improving motivation by increasing the variety of tasks and reducing monotony. Workers move from one task to another, either on the basis of a systematic rota worked out by management, or less formally on a job-swapping basis by agreement with co-workers.

❑ *Job enlargement* involves giving each employee a range of tasks as part of his normal pattern of working. This is sometimes known as horizontal job enlargement.

❑ *Job enrichment*, also known as vertical job enlargement, involves giving each worker additional roles such as inspection, supervision or after sales service.

❑ *Autonomous group working,* as the name implies, involves the creation of self-managed multi-skilled teams of workers responsible for more or less complete tasks such as vehicle assembly.

Autonomous working groups were pioneered in the automotive industry at Volvo in Sweden in the 1960s. A more recent example quoted by Tom Peters[4] is General Motors' Cadillac Plant at Livonia, Michigan.

The approach adopted there has the following characteristics:

1. Every employee is assigned to a small group of 8 to 15 people, known as a *business* team.

2. Each team develops its own indicators of its performance.

3. Each team meets weekly to review performance.

4. Most awards for suggestions reflect ideas put forward by teams.

5. Support for one's team counts in individual performance appraisal.

6. Job specialization has been more or less eliminated, and there is a 'pay-for-knowledge' incentive scheme to encourage employees to acquire new skills.

7. Second-line supervision (general foremen) has been completely eliminated, while the number of first-line foremen

has been reduced by 40 per cent and their job title
changed to that of team co-ordinator.

The most celebrated European examples of experiments in
job design have been at Philips (job enlargement), ICI (job
enrichment) and Volvo (autonomous work groups). While the
leading UK centre for research and ideas was the Tavistock
Institute, in the USA the leading advocates of improving motivation through job design have been Fred Herzberg, and Lou
Davis of the Center for the Quality of Working Life. The best
publicized US applications were in AT&T, which carried out
19 job enrichment projects in the 1960s, affecting over 1000
employees.

Among other US companies reporting beneficial results
from incorporating human factors considerations into job
design are Texas Instruments, PPG Industries, Monsanto,
Syntex, Oldsmobile Division of General Motors, Corning,
Alcan and Kaiser Aluminium.

The benefits have included reduced absenteeism, reduced
labour turnover, reduced overtime, reductions in staff numbers, increases in production, productivity and earnings,
reductions in supervision, increased sales, reduced wastage,
quality improvements, less sickness, and improved time-
keeping.

During the 1970s and early 1980s, interest in job design
and its relationship to motivation largely died away. This was
partly because the clear 'hard' short-term gains from the traditional task specialization – reductions in work in progress
and throughput times, reduced space requirements and sim-
plified production control – were believed to outweigh 'softer'
considerations of motivation and commitment. In addition,
'the Hawthorne effect' meant that initial gains in output or
quality from job enrichment experiments proved not always
to be sustainable. Finally, new attitudes and approaches to
employee motivation ensured that many of the principles of
job design that emerged from the research and well-publi-
cized experiments have been adopted as normal managerial
practice, so that forms of job enrichment are being practised
today as a matter of course.

More recently, however, interest is reviving, particularly in
North America, where some of the most successful attempts

to meet Japanese competition have involved radical changes in job design in order to raise levels of motivation and commitment.

REWARDS SYSTEMS AND MOTIVATION

Employee commitment is clearly a central issue when it comes to the design of the organization's rewards system. As always, in the sphere of organization design there are many approaches to choose from, and what works well in one situation can fail completely in another.

The Traditional Approach

The traditional approach to reward has been to relate pay and other benefits to characteristics of jobs, such as levels of skill or qualification required, level of responsibility carried, degree of danger involved, working conditions, and unsocial hours. Elaborate systems of job evaluation have been developed to enable comparisons and rankings of jobs to be carried out within organizations, while at the same time the evaluation of such characteristics in the wider society is reflected in the 'market rates' attached to various job classifications.

In traditional rewards systems of the kind found in bureaucracies, there is a pay rate or scale associated with each job, together with a differential allocation of the tangible or intangible rewards – such as level of pension benefit, private health insurance, company car and various symbols of status. Such rewards are relatively fixed, regardless of how well the job is performed, but benefits attached to a particular job frequently increase with length of service. The fairness or legitimacy of such systems is defended on the one hand by demonstrating their elaborate and comprehensive nature, and hence the 'objectivity' of the system of job evaluation in use, and on the other by pointing to the market rate for jobs in the outside world.

Such a system clearly does not address the issue of individual motivation to achieve outstanding performance. Either it

is assumed that individuals will be adequately motivated by
receiving rewards that are seen to be based on objective criteria, or it is believed that motivation is derived primarily
from quite different aspects of organizational life and that
provided there is no serious dissatisfaction with pay and benefits, these things are largely irrelevant from the viewpoint of
motivation.

Pay for Performance

Using this approach people are assigned a basic salary or
wage and rewards package on the basis of job classification,
but achieve annual monetary awards above this level as a
consequence of assessments of their contribution, performance or 'merit'. The perceived 'fairness' or legitimacy of this
approach depends on a number of factors. First, there is the
extent to which performance is capable of objective assessment or measurement. Jobs obviously vary to a considerable
extent in relation to this criterion. Secondly, the successful
completion of some tasks calls for a team effort. In such
instances it is very difficult to determine the relative contribution of individual team members. Thirdly, organization cultures vary a great deal – in some there is the kind of
individualistic culture in which individual merit pay is seen as
totally appropriate, whereas in other cultures the approach is
seen as destructive of teamwork.

Rosabeth Moss Kanter[5] points out that in a Conference
Board Survey, around 90 per cent of American companies
rated individual performance as the chief factor determining
pay increases, yet the majority of employees surveyed by the
Opinion Research Corporation saw little connection between
contribution and subsequent pay increases.

Some schemes are criticized on the grounds that the
increases are too small to be significant – 10 to 15 per cent of
basic salary is suggested as the threshold at which there
begins to be real reinforcement of high level performance.

Another weakness of such schemes is the reluctance shown
by managers and supervisors when it comes to making sharp
distinctions between the performance levels achieved by their
subordinates. They tend to take the easy way out and rate

virtually everybody 'above average'. Managers also tend to fight for high ratings for their own team members relative to those of other groups in the organization.

Profit-Related Pay (PRP)

The inclusion in the rewards package of a bonus reflecting company performance or profitability is a growing trend. Such one-time payments, because they do not increase basic salary, do not add to fixed costs. Moreover, in the UK they offer tax advantages.

The difficulties with this approach are obvious, however. First, there is no real link between individual effort or performance and reward. If the bonus is paid out to all employees, those who did an outstanding job receive no more than those who did the minimum short of being fired. Also, in a year in which a consumer boom or the failure of a competitor turns out to be the main cause for increased profits, where is the rationale for rewarding employees for their contribution? If the bonus is to be sufficiently large to affect motivation, is it justifiable to expect low-paid employees to put a significant proportion of their incomes at risk? When paying the mortgage is dependent upon the company achieving its profit targets in a recession year, the individual may feel powerless and alienated.

The number of employees covered by registered profit-related pay schemes in 1993 was over 1,500,000, which represented an increase of 28 per cent over the previous year.

SINGLE STATUS

In virtually every country of the world, non-manual or 'white collar' work has traditionally carried with it a higher status and better terms and conditions of work than manual or 'blue collar' work. This status divide has been particularly strong and durable in Britain. White collar status is reflected in hours of work, degree of job security, being salaried rather than hourly paid, enjoying better pension rights, sickness benefits and holidays, having incremental pay scales and in many instances separate canteen arrangements.

In the past two decades more and more organizations have come to see the status gap as an obstacle to establishing full trust and co-operation between management and shop-floor employees. In consequence there are now many examples of moves either partially or wholly to single status or harmonization of terms and conditions of employment for all workers.

Price[6] gives examples of successful single-status deals in the UK. One, at Tioxide UK in 1987, involved the withdrawal of recognition of the Transport and General Workers' Union, a totally new payments system including a profit-related element, and complete flexibility, with no demarcation between jobs.

At Johnson and Johnson, harmonization was carried out step by step between 1974 and 1982, as different aspects of conditions of employment such as pensions, holidays and sick pay arrangements were tackled in turn. Full harmonization followed, involving pay structures, replacing individual incentives for manual workers with across-the-board group incentives and profit-sharing schemes and the allocation of new responsibilities to supervisory staff.

Advantage is often taken of the opportunity of starting afresh on a greenfield site, as in the case of BICC Optical Cables at Whiston, where a seven-grade integrated pay structure covering all employees was introduced alongside common pay and performance review systems and harmonized conditions of employment.

Without doubt, many British firms as well as enterprises in other Western countries have been influenced by the success achieved by Japanese companies operating locally. Practice at companies like Nissan, Toshiba and Hitachi, such as no separate canteens or car parks, no distinctions of dress and a general absence of status 'perks', have been strongly linked to their achievement of harmonious labour relations and remarkably high standards of productivity and quality.

TRAINING AND COMMITMENT

Peters emphasizes the seriousness with which Japanese companies approach shop floor training and emphasizes that it is concerned as much with 'empowering' employees in the motivational sense as with the transfer of skills and technology. He argues that for most US and European organizations, motivation and job satisfaction are seen as being to do with keeping people contented, whereas for the Japanese it is to do with empowering them to transform performance. He quotes the example of the Nissan plant start-up in Smyrna, Tennessee, where $63 million was spent training 2000 workers – over $30,000 a head before a single car came off the line. It is hard to imagine many US or European organizations making such a huge investment in human capital.

The use of training primarily as a means for changing attitudes and building a committed workforce is, in any case, a relatively recent development. In Britain, large organizations such as British Airways and National Westminster Bank have provided training for all employees in the field of customer service. This training is not intended so much to impart specific job-related skills, but rather to instil in the participants an emotional commitment to service, to quality and to organizational success.

SECURITY OF EMPLOYMENT

It is characteristic of a number of high performance organizations, particularly in the US and Japan, but more rarely in Europe, that they offer a virtual guarantee of security of employment. In effect what they are doing is saying that all employees, and not just the management or the top executive team, have full membership in the organization and that once admitted to membership they have acquired rights, among which one of the most important is the right to security of employment.

The US firms which have had such policies in the past have included IBM, SC Johnson (of Johnson's Wax), Hewlett Packard, Hallmark, Digital and Federal Express. Some of these, however, have abandoned the attempt to guarantee security as a result of the difficult business conditions of the early 1990s.

Among the benefits of a sense of security on the part of the workforce are the following:

❏ A greater willingness to accept change, to volunteer ideas which raise productivity, and to give up restrictive practices.

❏ Co-operation and flexibility generally including a willingness to be retrained.

❏ Redundancy costs and the costs of recruiting and training 'green' labour when business picks up again are virtually eliminated.

Frequently, security of employment is accompanied by other features of organizational design which reinforce its motivational aspects. One which is particularly important is an employee share ownership plan (ESOP).

Employee Share Ownership

In the US, around 80 of the Fortune 500 top companies have introduced ESOPs. They are now in place in firms such as Procter and Gamble, ITT, Xerox and Delta.

PepsiCo became the first Fortune 500 company to introduce employee stock options. Each year, workers will get options equal to 10 per cent of their wages or salaries, priced at the stock's current value. Employees can exercise their options at any time within ten years after the options are granted. When they do, the company will pay out the profit in the form of Pepsi shares. If employees hold their stock rather than sell it, employee ownership will grow at a rate of about 4 per cent a decade.

In 1979 just 30 employee share schemes had been approved by the Inland Revenue in the UK. Now there are more than 4000, covering 1.5 million workers.

COMMITMENT AND CULTURE

The view is rapidly gaining ground that corporate culture has an even more powerful influence on employee motivation than structural factors such as the design of jobs or work groups or systems such as incentive schemes. This view reflects the spectacular successes achieved by certain companies with strong and distinctive cultures and where there is convincing evidence that the success largely reflects an unusually high level of employee commitment and motivation.

Tom Peters has publicized a number of American examples in a whole series of books and videos featuring a wide range of organizations in terms of size, industry, public and private sector and ownership. Peters' US models include Apple Computers, Cray Research, Federal Express, The Limited, Milliken, Stew Leonard's Supermarket, Johnsonville Sausage and Worthington Industries.

In Britain the creation of a service culture was central to the improvement in British Airways' performance, and many organizations are now trying (not always successfully) to emulate this achievement by means of cultural change.

What kind of culture is it that can have a radical effect on the attitudes and commitment of employees? The answer appears to lie primarily in the sphere of values. Employees are 'turned on' and become committed when:

❑   The values are clearly articulated and they are constantly reinforced.

❑   The values are ones they can identify with and adopt as their own.

❑   Top management 'lives' the values.

At the beginning of this chapter the example of the Procter and Gamble plant showed how effective values can be. In this case every employee carried a statement of values around with him or her in the form of a plastic card.

Other companies express their core values much more succinctly – British Airways uses the expression 'Putting people first'. Thomas J. Watson, founder of IBM, argued that

> the basic philosophy, spirit and drive of an organization have far more to do with its relative achievements than do technological or economic resources, organizational structures, innovation and timing. All these things weigh heavily on success but they are, I think, transcended by how strongly the people in the organization believe in its basic precepts and how faithfully they carry them out.

The Importance of a Sense of Mission

Andrew Campbell and his co-researchers at the Ashridge Strategic Management Centre[7] have carried out a broadly based study of company practice in using mission statements. They found that for many companies, a mission statement was simply a way of stating the organization's business goals. For others, however, it was a much more philosophical declaration concerned with values. They argue that mission should ideally appeal both to the minds (strategy) and the hearts (values and beliefs) of employees.

Their model of the ideal mission statement has four elements:

1. *Purpose – what is the company for?*   Where the purpose points to some higher goals as well as commercial success, the potential for motivating people is obvious. For example, George Merck, son of the founder of Merck, the world's largest pharmaceutical company, said 'Medicine is for the patients. It is not for the profits. The profits follow and if we have remembered that they have never failed to appear'.

2. *Strategy – indicating how the purpose is to be achieved.*

3. *Behaviour standards*   The standards of performance and patterns of behaviour that will be involved in implementing the strategy. In British Airways the purpose was to become 'The world's favourite airline'. The strategy for achieving this was the provision of exceptional customer service. This was then translated into performance standards and behaviours, mainly in training at every level from the board down.

4. *Values*   These are the underlying beliefs which give a moral force to the other aspects of the mission.

Campbell and his colleagues point out, however, that merely writing and issuing a mission statement does not itself create a strong sense of mission.

Building Commitment at Rover

The successful drive to restore the fortunes of the Rover car company in recent years was based on the achievement of a reputation for build quality, which in turn required the full commitment of the workforce.

In the mid-1980s, with the appointment of a new top management team and the forging of the partnership with Honda, the quality initiative began with the theme 'Working with Pride'. At the time it was believed that improvements in communications, suggestion schemes and training would be capable of bringing about the necessary level of commitment. This was subsequently recognized to have been a mistaken view, but much was learned from the company's first employee attitude survey, conducted in 1986. This showed that the company's systems, procedures and style of management were all acting as barriers to the achievement of consistent high quality. It was realized that radical change was needed and a new total quality improvement (TQI) programme was launched in early 1987.

David Bower, Rover's Personnel Director has given a very full account of what was subsequently done to build commitment.[8]

The first phase included a major training initiative to provide awareness of TQI principles and practices. Three hundred senior managers, including board directors, attended four-day courses in 1987 and 4000 managers and supervisors were trained in the next two years. TQI training for all remaining employees started in January 1989 and was completed by the end of 1991. In 1989 the Rover Group mission was conceived: 'To be internationally renowned for extraordinary customer satisfaction'.

Over 600 local groups – 'quality action teams' – led by managers and voluntary shop-floor discussion groups (Rover's name for quality circles) were established, and in 1990 the organization structure was changed from a functional basis to one based on six business units.

Eleven levels in the hierarchy were reduced to six. The traditional role of foreman was abolished and replaced with team leader roles.

Greater emphasis, however, was placed on the need to change processes and culture. 'Rover Learning Business' was created in 1990 in order to stimulate the process of organizational learning. This is a 'business within a business'. Its goal is to provide a top quality learning and development service to all employees as customers, regardless of location and with equality of opportunity.

Given the development of a more open culture encouraging individual development and involvement, a fresh approach to the basic assumptions underlying conditions of employment was called for. This, known as 'Rover Tomorrow – The New Deal', was accepted by the workforce and came into operation in April 1992.

The Rover case illustrates the use of a wide range of approaches – changes to the organization structure, new processes and procedures from remuneration to training and culture change – as part of a successful drive to develop a high level of commitment to company objectives in a workforce previously marked by apathy and alienation.

SUMMARY

Employee motivation and commitment is the outcome of a number of influences, the main ones being:

❑ The intrinsic satisfactions associated with the nature of the work itself.

❑ The cohesiveness and autonomy of working groups.

❑ The particular system of reward and remuneration adopted by the organization, including performance-related pay, profit sharing and employee share ownership.

❑ Single status – the absence of an 'us and them' divide between managers and workers.

❑ Specific devices aimed at involving shopfloor employees in decision-making, such as quality circles.

❑ Training and development.

❑ Security of employment.

❏   A strong corporate culture which is associated with values people can identify with.

❏   The creation of a strong sense of mission.

Almost all of the above approaches were adopted by the Rover Group in building a high level of commitment to quality in the 1980s and early 1990s.

References

1. Taylor, F W (1911) *The   Principles   of   Scientific Management*, Harper & Row, New York.

2. Herzberg, F (1966) *Work and the Nature of Man*, World, Cleveland, Ohio.

3. Emery, F, 'The Democratization of the Workplace', *Manpower and Applied Psychology*, Vol 1, 1967.

4. Peters, T (1987) *Thriving on Chaos*, Macmillan, Basingstoke.

5. Kanter, R M (1989) *When Giants Learn to Dance*, Simon & Schuster, New York.

6. Price, R (1989) 'The Decline and Fall of the Status Divide' in K. Sisson (ed.) *Personnel Management in Britain*, Blackwell, Oxford.

7. Campbell, A, Devine, M and Young, D (1993) *A Sense of Mission*, FT/Pitman, London.

8. Bower, D in Sadler, P (ed.) (1993) *Learning More About Learning Organizations*, AMED, London.

6
CO-ORDINATION – BUILDING THE SEAMLESS ORGANIZATION

The fair test of business administration, of industrial organization is whether you have a business with all its parts so co-ordinated, so moving together in their closely knit and adjusting activities, so linking, interlocking, inter-relating, that they make a working unit, not a congeries of separate pieces.

Mary Parker Follett

INTRODUCTION

This chapter deals with two interrelated issues. The first, co-ordination of activity, is the process of ensuring that activities of individuals or groups which are interdependent are carried out in such a way that they complement each other and thus make an optimum contribution to the achievement of the objectives of the organization as a whole. The second concerns the deeper, underlying psychological and social processes of welding the highly differentiated and specialized parts of an organization into a cohesive whole.

CO-ORDINATION OF ACTIVITY

Co-ordination is called for when there is a high degree of task interdependence – in other words, in those cases where the ability of one individual, group or division to carry out a task is dependent on the way another individual, group or division carries out some other, related task. There are three main types of task interdependence: sequential, reciprocal and shared resources.

Sequential interdependence exists where one person, group or division cannot perform a task until another person, group or division has performed a task occurring at an earlier stage in the production process. At department level this is exemplified by the interdependence of sales and production. At the work group or individual level it can clearly be seen in the sequence of operations on a typical assembly line.

Reciprocal interdependence exists where two or more individuals, groups or divisions have to interact simultaneously in order to accomplish a task. Reciprocal interdependence between groups can be seen for example when two or more departments of a company have to work in very close collaboration in order to fulfil a particular customer contract. Reciprocal interdependence between individuals within a group can be seen any Saturday afternoon on the football field.

Interdependence due to the common use of shared resources exists in cases where different individuals or groups need access to a common facility – a building or a piece of equipment – in order to do their work, with the result that their claims on the resource, which would otherwise lead to conflict, need to be co-ordinated.

Means of Achieving Co-ordination

Co-ordination can be achieved in a variety of ways and the choice of means will have important implications for organization design.

Co-ordination Through Line Management

Where the individuals, groups or divisions needing to be co-ordinated report to the same manager, the simplest method for achieving co-ordination is to make it part of that manager's responsibilities.

Co-ordination Through Staff Specialists

In many cases the activities requiring to be co-ordinated cross a number of organizational boundaries. In such cases one solution is to require co-ordination to be carried out by line management at progressively higher levels until, at the level of the chief executive, it absorbs a considerable proportion of the available time. An alternative is to set up positions or departments whose job it is to achieve co-ordination. Individual positions with this type of responsibility are variously called progress chasers, expeditors or liaison officers. Departments carry such titles as 'production scheduling' or 'new product development'.

Co-ordination Through the Grouping of Tasks

Another obvious way of achieving co-ordination is by grouping together in divisions or departments all those activities which need to be closely co-ordinated. Most sizeable companies which offer more than one product or service or which operate in more than one market find the complexity of activities is such that they have to abandon a functional type of organization structure in favour of one which groups people from different functions around a common task or purpose. This task or purpose can relate to a particular product, a particular market, or a particular geographical area. The requirements of co-ordination will not, however, be the sole determinant of the way in which people are grouped together, and this aspect of organization design will be discussed at greater length later in this chapter.

**Manufacturing of tape products at 3M –
improved co-ordination leading to increased efficiency**

Tape is made by coating a backing with adhesive and creating a giant roll. At one time these large rolls were then taken to slitting machines in another department at the other end of the factory. The two operations had separate supervisors. Co-ordination was poor and the result was hundreds of rolls stockpiled all over the place. Quality was the responsibility of quality control inspectors, and fell below acceptable levels.

Now coaters and slitters work side by side. Supervision is by product line, not by function – a supervisor for all masking tape operations, for example. Quality is the responsibility of individual operatives. Inventory has been cut dramatically, quality has improved, and manufacturing productivity has increased by two-thirds.

TEAMWORKING

Katzenbach and Smith[1] define a team as a 'small number of people with complementary skills who are committed to a common purpose, set of performance goals, and approach for which they hold themselves mutually accountable'. The distinction between a team and an ordinary working group lies in the ideas of mutuality, reciprocity and common commitment. A team is much more than a group of individuals with a common task. The process of teambuilding is to take a group of individuals who share a common task (such as the England soccer XI) and to transform them into a team such that their mutual understanding and their common commitment to victory play a more important part in their results than their individual skills.

The nature of the mutual understanding and reciprocal relationships involved in teamwork place a natural limitation on the size of a team – the maximum is about 16.

Clearly the requirement for teamworking is a function of the nature of the task and the degree of interdependence involved.

For the purposes of achieving co-ordination across internal organization boundaries, team members are, of course, drawn from different functions, disciplines or other parts of the organization. These teams – usually known as project groups, task forces or working parties, are quite different from other types of team such as autonomous working groups at shop-floor level.

The most important processes which will determine the success or otherwise of such teams include the following:

1. Careful selection of team members. Attention needs to be paid not only to the particular skill, competence or experience of each member, but also to his or her interpersonal skills and 'fit' with roles which the team needs.

2. The roles to be played if the team is to be fully effective. The best known and most often used set of team roles has been developed by Belbin.[2] He showed that people contribute to teams in some combination of three modes. The first is by contributing ideas, the second is by being sup-

portive and effective in interpersonal relationships and the third is by focusing on the task and its implementation. He identified nine roles as follows:

— plant

— shaper

— resource investigator

— co-ordinator

— teamworker

— implementer

— specialist

— monitor/evaluator

— completer/finisher.

3. The rapid development of mutual trust, respect and positive regard. This implies, first, that early meetings should be both frequent and not too rushed, allowing time for social process as well as the conduct of business and, secondly, that time should be found for purely social interaction away from the job.

4. Setting from the outset some clear rules of behaviour. These should cover such things as attendance at meetings, constructive confrontation, sharing of workload, procedures for inclusion of new members and for exclusion, common values, etc.

5. Establishing challenging and demanding performance standards and behaviour requirements.

6. Agreeing the process for arriving at and accepting team decisions.

7. Agreeing how the team is to be served with leadership.

8. Identifying some short-term objectives to test the team's ability to function.

9. Agreeing how the team's effectiveness is to be monitored and evaluated.

10. Maintaining strong connections with the rest of the organization – communicating progress and, even more important, ensuring that the team is open to and receptive to ideas from outside. It is vital to avoid the 'sealed room' syndrome in which a project group meets behind closed doors eventually producing a report which tells others what they should be thinking and doing and which inevitably ends up on a shelf gathering dust.

THE 'LOGICORP' CASE – CO-ORDINATION TO SUPPORT CREATIVITY

Colin Hastings and his co-authors[3] provide a clear example of teamworking across departments with the case of 'Logicorp'. The company manufactures and installs electronic surveillance equipment. It had enjoyed rapid growth on a single site over a 10-year period, reaching 1000 employees. Then, through acquisition and the opening of overseas subsidiaries, its size doubled in a single year. The projections were for doubling again in each of the two following years and for at least 10 sites across the world.

The company was determined to preserve some aspects of the way it worked despite its greater size. In particular it wished to maintain the ability of individual employees to identify with the organization's success; the informal nature of inter-departmental networking; and attitudes which encouraged creativity and innovation.

In order to achieve these objectives the company set up two kinds of team:

1. Inter-departmental teams, working on operational problems spanning departments.

2. Task forces, working on strategic, policy and organizational issues.

Training in teamworking skills was provided for the members of these teams, which then worked through the following four stages of activity over a three to six-month period.

1. Negotiating success criteria with project sponsors.

2. Exploring the problem and arriving at solutions.

3. Reporting to the Board and winning approval.

4. Setting up an implementation programme and in many instances managing the implementation process.

Among the topics tackled by the 'Logicorp' teams were:

1. What new businesses should the company be in in seven to 10 years' time, in order to meet its growth objectives?

2. How should the company be structured so as to sustain innovation and motivation?

3. How best to meet the information needs of the board.

4. How to improve the quality of customer service.

NETWORKING, USING INFORMATION TECHNOLOGY

An increasingly common method of achieving co-ordination between different parts of the organization, particularly when these are in different locations or different countries, is by means of networking using electronic mail. Where terminals are available to staff at many different levels, the result can be an organic system of interaction, involving networks within networks, temporary informal task groups, and 'dynamic coalitions'.

MATRIX ORGANIZATION

The term 'matrix management' was first used in the 1960s to describe a structure which had existed for some time in various organizations under other names. It began to attract interest, and its use spread in the late 1960s and early 1970s, since it seemed to offer a solution to some real problems.

For example, companies in the US aerospace industry which were functionally organized were required, in order to tender for government contracts, to submit organization charts showing that they had developed a project management system. Rather than abandon their basic functional structures, the idea of positioning a set of project groups alongside a set of functional departments in a grid or matrix had strong appeal. In this context the matrix structure represents a compromise between two sets of needs – the need felt by the customer (and sometimes also by the chief executive) for clear accountability for the success of a project, and the company's need for strong specialist departments with high standards of professional or technical expertise.

In essence, the matrix structure has emerged as a solution to growing complexity – the need to cope with more than one source of diversity simultaneously – different products, in different markets with different technologies. Complexity creates information overload, which can be dealt with in a number of ways – by decentralization of decision-making, by installing highly sophisticated computerized information systems, or by creating slack resources – buffer stocks or pools of manpower. The matrix offers an alternative approach by creating lateral relationships which cut across conventional vertical lines of authority. Some enthusiasts see the matrix as the model for the organization of the future. Others see it as an expensive, over-elaborate and confusing arrangement.

The enthusiasts are often attracted by the opportunities it offers to escape from the shackles of traditional hierarchical forms of organization by working in teams in which rank and seniority count for little, compared with expertise and ideas.

Those who argue against it draw attention to the fact that an inescapable feature of this structure is that each person has at least two bosses and has membership in at least two groups. This can create conflict and confusion. It certainly breaks one of the golden rules of classical management theory – the principle of unity of command.

In practice, matrix organizations are found primarily in aerospace companies, research and development organizations, large multifunctional organizations seeking to give equal attention to products or markets as to functions, management consultants and other forms of consultancy, the construction industry, advertising agencies and business schools.

Some of the problems associated with the operation of a matrix structure are:

❏ *Intrinsic instability* At one extreme there is a pull towards small, self-contained interdisciplinary teams, and at the other a pressure towards the concentration of precious functional expertise. The ensuing tug of war can eventually pull the structure in one direction or the other, while in the meantime it burns up considerable time and energy which would be better spent getting the job done.

❏ *Delay* Unless the culture of the enterprise favours risk-taking, decisions get pushed up the structure until a cross-over point is reached where authority clearly resides. This can delay and distort decision making.

❏ *Ambiguity* Individuals often experience difficulty in handling the ambiguity and uncertainty about such things as role, status and authority.

Kenneth Knight[4] gives an excellent summing up of the pros and cons of matrix management, using the criteria of efficiency, control and accountability, co-ordination, adaptation, and 'social effectiveness':

❏ *Efficiency* Matrix structures can maintain or increase efficiency in cases where key resources are distributed among sub-units, but the introduction of matrix structures into very rigid formal organizations can actually reduce efficiency.

❏ *Control and accountability* These can be readily achieved both in respect of the efficient use of resources and the accomplishment of task objectives in organizations using matrix structures.

❏ *Co-ordination* This is achieved through matrix structures, but expensively so and such structures are, therefore, only justified in situations where there is a high degree of interdependence against tight deadlines and strict technical or other specifications.

❏ *Adaptation* This is facilitated by the matrix organization through its ability to enable the rapid exchange of information and ideas laterally and diagonally through the structure.

❑ *Social effectiveness*   This is limited, since matrix structures tend to generate stress, confusion and conflict.

Co-ordination by Committee

This is probably the least effective means of achieving co-ordination between different groups within the same organization. The weaknesses of committees are well-known. They include:

❑ Members attend as representatives of their departments or functions. Their minds are set not on achieving smooth co-operation, so much as protecting departmental interests or competing for resources.

❑ Committee effectiveness is lowered by failings in chairmanship. In particular, where the chairman is drawn from one of the activity areas to be co-ordinated, he or she can be open to the charge of bias; weak chairmanship can lead to time-wasting and poor quality decision-making.

❑ Committees are notoriously uneconomic when their outputs are measured against the man-hours involved in them.

❑ Committees tend to compromise between conflicting interests, rather than make optimal decisions, or accept risks. They involve the very real danger of 'group-think'.

❑ Getting the right people together for meetings is notoriously difficult, with the result that meetings are subject to cancellation or are spaced apart. This inevitably slows down decision-making.

IMPLICATIONS FOR ORGANIZATION DESIGN

Bearing in mind that the requirements of co-ordination cannot be treated in isolation from the other objectives of the design process, then the following procedure is suggested:

❑ Identify those activities which really do need to be closely co-ordinated and consider the advantages and disadvantages of grouping them into organizational units.

❑ Where such activities *are* grouped into single organizational units, select appropriate processes for ensuring that co-ordination takes place:

— team-building activities

— group bonuses

❑ Where co-ordination requirements between groups continue to exist, select the appropriate processes for achieving co-ordination:

— making higher level line management responsible

— creating project groups or task forces

— appointing liaison officers

— creating specialist staff

— creating matrix structures

❑ Whereas committees can be useful for certain purposes (such as health and safety committees), seriously consider abolishing all committees which have been set up in order to achieve co-ordination between departments, since it is highly probable that they are not cost effective.

Co-ordination at Corporate Level

The objectives of co-ordination at corporate level include the following:

1. Ensuring that different subsidiaries or divisions of the organization are contributing to the objectives of the organization as a whole.

2. Achieving economies in the use of resources – for example, through common purchasing policies.

3. Ensuring the supply of future top management for the corporation through the co-ordination of 'high flyer' management development programmes.

4. Resolving conflicting claims on capital for investment programmes.

5. Agreeing transfer prices where appropriate.

6. Transferring best practice from one part of the organization to another.

The difficulty and the cost of achieving co-ordination grows proportionately to the increase of diversity of the activities requiring to be co-ordinated.

The principal sources of differentiation are, of course, functions, products, markets and territories.

What Companies Do In Practice

John Daniels and colleagues[5] studied the organization structures of 37 US firms with both high product diversity *and* high dependence on foreign sales. The researchers set up and tested a number of hypotheses:

1. *Few if any firms handle foreign operations through functional structures*   Only two firms used a functional structure – but these were oil companies, having many products but being vertically integrated and essentially based on a single product – oil.

2. *Few use matrix structures*   Only one did so. (The unity of command principle is perhaps too well established.)

3. *As complexity grows, global product structures will be found more frequently than international division structures*   This was found to be true if diversity of products is looked at, but not true if the criterion is dependence on foreign sales.

4. *Some firms will stick to international division structures, despite very high levels of product diversity and dependence on foreign sales*   Yes, true. They cope by using other devices such as committees, task forces, changed rewards systems, and strong articulation of corporate goals.

5. *Conglomerates (ie companies with unrelated products) use product divisions more than companies with related products*   Very true.

6. *Firms with international division structures invest more in R & D than companies with product structures*   Not verified.

7. *Firms with area division structures depend more on foreign sales than firms with either international or product division structures*   Not significant.

Research carried out by Egelhoff[*] of Columbia University involved studying the relationships between strategy and structure in the 50 largest companies in the following industries:*

❑   vehicle manufacturing

❑   electrical equipment

❑   telecommunications equipment

❑   chemicals

❑   pharmaceuticals

❑   consumer packaged goods

❑   tyres.

As well as looking at functional, product-based and geographical structures Egelhoff included firms in which all foreign subsidiaries reported to an international division which was structurally separate from a domestic division.

His findings were as follows:

❑   Companies with functional structures had relatively narrow product ranges overseas and there were few differences or modifications to the products from one country to another. They tended to have relatively few foreign subsidiaries, a low level of outside ownership of foreign subsidiaries and had made few foreign acquisitions.

❑   Companies with international and domestic divisions had relatively small foreign operations and relatively few foreign subsidiaries.

❑   Companies with geographical divisions had relatively

---

* (Plus three companies not drawn from these industries.)

large foreign operations, a high level of foreign manufacturing, and a large number of foreign subsidiaries.

❏ Finally, companies with product divisions tended to have a wide range of products on sale in foreign countries, a high rate of new product development, relatively large foreign operations and a relatively large number of foreign subsidiaries.

Companies typically manage international operations through an international division in the early stages. Subsequently, companies with limited product diversity typically adopt an area structure, while companies with considerable product diversity and a high volume of foreign sales adopt a matrix structure.

Although the global matrix appeared to offer the perfect solution, for many companies the result was disappointing – 'the promised land of the global matrix turned out to be an organizational quagmire from which they were forced to retreat'.

Dow Chemical, one of the companies to pioneer the global matrix, eventually returned to a more conventional structure with clear lines of responsibility assigned to area managers. Citibank also abandoned the matrix after experimenting with it for several years.

The main difficulties encountered were:

❏ Decision processes which were slow, costly and acrimonious.

❏ Energy sapped by constant travelling and frequent meetings.

Bartlett and Ghoshal[7] quote one senior executive among those whom they interviewed who perceptively said that the problem was not so much how to change the organization structure into a matrix but how to create a matrix in the minds of managers.

THE CASE OF PROCTER AND GAMBLE

Bartlett and Ghoshal provide an interesting account of the evolution of structure in Procter and Gamble.

Until the 1950s, Procter and Gamble's structure was a simple functional one, with the marketing function dominant. Sales were concentrated in the US. Overseas operations were relatively small and were confined to the UK and Canada.

In 1955 the domestic operation was divisionalized by product – detergents, personal products and food products.

In the late 1950s, as international growth occurred the international side was structured around geographical markets. The functional influence on local companies remained strong, particularly in marketing where brand management, extensive market research and product testing were universally imposed practices. There was, however, no strong integration of product strategies.

In the 1970s, problems were caused by rising raw materials costs, checks to the growth of consumer spending and intensified competition. The need for a more co-ordinated product strategy was felt.

In the late 1970s the company strengthened its European R & D facility and organized it along product lines. 'Euroteams' were established to achieve new product development on a Europe-wide basis. The results included such famous brands as Ariel soap powder, Fairy dishwashing liquid and Camay soap.

Subsequently 'Euro Brand Teams' were developed, comprising brand and advertising managers from local subsidiaries, key functional managers from head office and led by the general manager of the subsidiary chosen to be the lead company for that particular brand.

In the 1980s, as product innovation became an increasingly important competitive weapon in global markets, R & D in the US was also strengthened and reorganized into 'product streams'.

THE UNITECH CASE

Unitech plc is an industrial group which had a turnover in 1987/88 of £217 millions.

It defined the business it was in as being 'to supply the industrial electronics market with components and sub-assemblies'. It manufactured its own products as well as distributing the products of other manufacturers.

Where the technology was most advanced and the capital investment needed to get into manufacturing was normally highest, Unitech engaged in distribution. In the case of medium- to low-technology products, it became involved in manufacturing.

The group's major customers were the leading electronics manufacturers in the main industrialized countries. It selected the markets in which it operated not only on the grounds of profitability but also because they offered opportunities for relatively small companies to win a significant market share.

Origins of the Company

Peter Curry read Engineering at Oxford and was trained in management at Harvard Business School. He had always wanted to start his own business and the opportunity arose in 1962 when he was 31, with the option to purchase 55 per cent of a small business (Coutant Electronics) manufacturing power supply systems. He raised the £25,000 needed, with the assistance of Gordon McPherson whom he had met at Harvard and who was a partner with Buckmaster and Moore. Unitech was formed as a company with a share capital of £100,000, of which 30 per cent was called, providing £5000 for running expenses as well as the £25,000 to purchase a controlling interest in Coutant. The new company was formed by Slaughter and May, and its chairman until 1970 was Peter Lumsden, a partner in Buckmaster and Moore. Gordon McPherson joined the board. Later, when the company went public in 1971, Tommy Walmsley, a partner in Slaughter and May, also joined the board. In the early years Curry was employed by Buckmaster and Moore for 75 per cent of his time, devoting the other 25 per cent to the new company which he ran from his Buckmaster and Moore office. In 1966 Peter Curry's brother John joined the company after qualifying as an accountant and getting his MBA from Harvard, and was appointed to the board in 1970. John resigned as an executive director in 1987 in order to start his own business. He remained on the board in a non-executive capacity.

How the Company Developed

Over the next seven or so years, Curry started one or two new businesses a year, using his intimate knowledge of the electronics industry to spot gaps in the market during a period of rapidly changing technology. He moved into the distribution business by winning the agency for Motorola products in the UK. In 1969 the strategy was changed in one important respect. The venture capital approach adopted thus far and involving starting up new businesses or investing in 'fledgling' businesses resulted in a negative cash flow, with a consequent need to keep raising capital. At this time the equity market was turning down and the image of venture capital companies was becoming tarnished. Unitech always sought a majority interest in the companies in which it invested, and the consolidation of losses in the Unitech accounts reduced the value of Unitech shares while new business was building market share and profitability. Another growing problem at this time was the disproportionate amount of management effort absorbed by small start-up businesses. In view of these factors, Curry decided to change his approach and to concentrate on acquiring established companies.

The Company's Objectives

These were very clear. They were the achievement of a 40 per cent return (before tax) on capital employed and a 20 per cent per annum compound growth rate. (The former is what is needed to finance the latter). Most companies avoid cash flow problems by having low growth coupled with excess assets. Unitech had high growth and no excess assets, so was constantly needing cash and came under pressure if the growth objective was achieved, but not the rate of return. There was no wider statement of objectives.

Sales Breakdown

The sales for 1987/8 were made up as follows:

By product	Distribution	{	Systems	28%
			Semiconductors	14%
	Agency			14%
	Manufacturing	{	Connectors	12%
			Power supplies	14%
			Control products	13%
			Special products	5%
By market			Industrial	33%
			Data processing	26%
			Telecommunications	19%
			Defence	15%
			Others	7%
By region			UK	51%
			Europe	38%
			USA	11%

The Business Units

At this time the group consisted of 25 companies, each employing between 100 and 500 employees. They were located as follows:

	UK	Continent	N. America	Far East
Manufacturing				
Power Supplies	2	1	1	-
Connectors	2	3	3	-
Controls	2	2	2	-
Special products	2	-	-	-
Distribution	2	2	1	-
	10	8	7	-

Table 6.1 shows the results achieved in terms of sales and profits over the previous decade.

Table 6.1 *Unitech's financial results, 1979–88 (£000s)*

	Sales	Profit before tax	Net profit after tax
1979	45,857	3,560	2,836
1980	71,812	5,262	4,431
1981	86,956	4,266	3,307
1982	89,424	3,782	2,055
1983	115,806	5,872	3,204
1984	154,118	13,111	7,703
1985	204,714	15,020	8,888
1986	198,285	10,730	6,449
1987	215,853	13,575	9,011
1988	217,286	14,738	9,362

Organizational Choice

The choices here were clear. Top management could, in theory, choose between the following alternatives:

A Functional Structure

Manufacturing and marketing/sales activities of all companies would be co-ordinated by the centre. The advantages of such an approach would include the opportunity to rationalize production; to transfer best practice in manufacturing across companies; purchasing economies related to scale of operations; well co-ordinated policies for market penetration; co-ordination of selling activities and global promotion of a Unitech brand.

The negative aspects would include loss of local knowledge and flexibility, loss of some valuable entrepreneurial local management due to loss of autonomy, and additional costs of corporate staffs.

A Structure Based on Markets Served

This would involve grouping companies in terms of their main markets such as defence, telecommunications, computer manufacturers etc.

Although this option might appear attractive, in that it would ensure a strong focus on the needs of particular customers, it would be difficult to achieve in practice since many of the companies which had been acquired over the years served several different market segments.

A Structure Based on Products

This would involve grouping companies according to the products being manufactured, with distribution as a separate activity.

The advantages would include the sharing of product knowledge across companies, a strong focus on product development, and, because at least some products link with particular market segments, a strong customer focus also. This option would offer the possibility of an overall Unitech brand, or of keeping the separate brands and corporate identities of individual companies. A 'loose rein' approach to the management of product divisions would ensure responsiveness to local conditions and local managerial autonomy remained high.

Negative aspects of this approach might have included the encouragement of a 'not invented here' attitude in individual companies, and duplication of effort by sales forces.

A Structure Based on Geography

The natural choice here would have involved creating three main divisions – the UK, continental Europe and North America, plus an embryonic Far East division. The obvious advantages would have been to move decision-making to geographical markets, which would be important if regional and national political, economic and cultural factors were of considerable significance in these particular markets.

On the negative side, this would have involved dilution of product knowledge and might have generated internal conflicts based on national rivalry.

The Company Solution

In practice, the company opted for a product-based divisional structure, as shown in Fig. 6.1.

Seven executive positions reported direct to the chief executive (who was also chairman of the company). Three were responsible for functions – finance, strategic development and human resources – and four were directors of operating divisions – power supplies, control products and connectors combined with special products constituted three manufacturing decisions, while a fourth director co-ordinated all the distribution companies. (In practice there were six direct reports – one director was responsible both for the strategic development function and the connectors/special products operation).

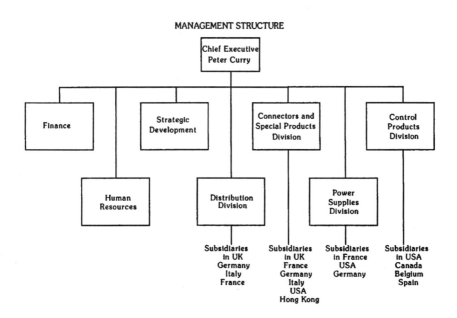

Figure 6.1 *Unitech plc – organization chart, 1988*

Strategic Change Leads to Organizational Change

The 1988/89 financial year was the most significant in Unitech's history. Veeco Instruments Inc was acquired for £180 million. Although its name suggests its main activity was in the field of instrument manufacture, Veeco, through its Lambda subsidiaries, was in fact principally a manufacturer of power supplies based in the USA, with major subsidiaries in Japan and Europe. This acquisition made Unitech the world's largest manufacturer of power supplies.

The acquisition was financed partly with cash (arising from the sale of new shares to Elektrowatt of Switzerland, which raised £50 million) and partly with debt. A large part of this debt was repaid through the sale of Unitech's distribution activities for £55 million. The balance was financed by debt, which was subsequently reduced by the sale of Veeco's instrument division to its management for £18 million.

The Lambda name had been the recognized world market leader in power supplies for many years. Its strength in the USA and Japan complemented Unitech's strength in Britain and continental Europe. Unitech now concentrated on manufacturing components and sub-assemblies for industrial electronic equipment manufacturers.

During the year, Wells Electronics Inc (USA) was also acquired for £12 million, financed by a vendor placing at 313p per share. The company makes burn-in and test sockets.

The results for the six months ending 30 November 1989 showed the impact of these strategic moves. Sales rose from £115 million in the corresponding half year in 1988 to £153 million, and trading profit rose dramatically from £7¼ million to £12¼million. However, interest charges of £4¼ million (compared with interest income of £½ million in 1988) and income from minority interests of £1¼ million left a net profit of £7¾ million. The number of employees rose from 3200 to 6200.

Unitech's new subsidiary had a tradition of strong functional management with a high level of co-ordination of manufacturing and marketing from the centre. The exception to this was its relationship with the Japanese company in which it held a majority interest and which was accorded considerable autonomy under the leadership of its entrepreneurial founder.

Clearly, the inclusion into the Unitech group of this very sizeable company with its UK base and global presence necessitated major structural change in the company as a whole.

The solution adopted is shown in Fig. 6.2. Basically there are now two product divisions – one, based in the US, manufactures power supplies. The other, with its managing director based in the UK, co-ordinates all other manufacturing operations worldwide, but operates on the same 'loose-rein' approach with a high degree of local autonomy as in the previous Unitech structure.

Although this new structure is basically a product-based structure it now has strong elements of a regional structure as well. For it to work effectively involves creating a sense of teamwork between the key people in top management positions and, in Bartlett and Ghoshal's words, 'creating the matrix in their minds'.

INTEGRATION – CREATING THE 'SEAMLESS' ORGANIZATION

This is the process of binding together the various parts of an organization into a cohesive whole. It is a more general, more diffused process than co-ordination of activities, which relates to specific identifiable task interdependencies. It has more to do with states of mind and attitudes than with concrete activities and behaviours.

By definition, integration is the process of bringing together individuals or groups who have hitherto been differentiated or separated in some way. The most common forces in organizations which pull people apart from each other and distract them from focusing on the goals of the organization as a whole are:

❑ Functional or geographical boundaries, between different specializations between line and staff or between different areas.

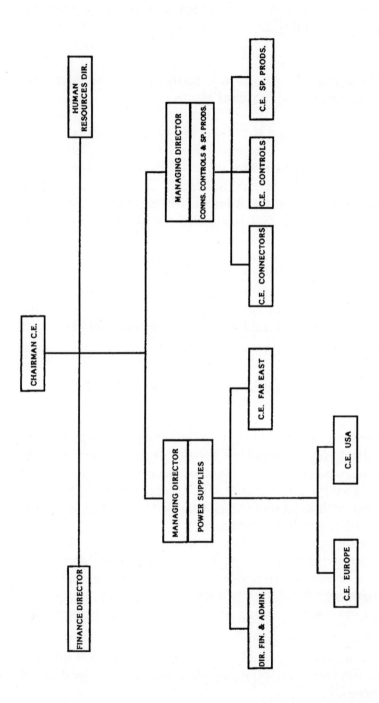

Figure 6.2 *Unitech plc – reorganization, 1989*

❑ Hierarchical boundaries, especially those between monthly-paid staff (white collar workers) and weekly-paid employees (blue collar workers) and between people in head office and those in operating divisions and subsidiaries.

❑ Historically derived boundaries, usually following mergers, separating people according to which party to the merger or acquisition they originally belonged to. (In the British confectionery/soft drink manufacturer Cadbury Schweppes, for example, there is still a clearly visible boundary between Cadbury people and Schweppes people after some 20 years.)

Approaches to integration can include:

❑ Abolishing the boundaries, by either:

— as far as possible, grouping together people from different functions in multi-disciplinary teams, either permanently or in project groups or matrix structures;

— moving as rapidly as possible towards single status by abolishing all the traditional and operationally quite unnecessary distinctions of class and status between blue and white collar workers. Make everyone a monthly-paid, salaried employee, laying down the same hours of work and conditions of employment (sickness pay, pensions, etc) for everyone. Do away with separate lunch facilities, separate toilets or separate entrances. (In the context of British society this will not be easy, nor capable of being achieved overnight. Expect as much resistance from blue collar employees as from those in white collar jobs. It *can* be done in Britain, however, as companies like IBM and Sony have clearly demonstrated.)

❑ Moving people backwards and forwards freely across the boundaries that cannot be broken down, by encouraging social interaction, sports events and other opportunities to meet and mix.

❑ Using training programmes at all levels from induction courses through to top management seminars to reinforce a feeling of identification with the firm.

❑ Linking people throughout the organization through the emotional and psychological bonds of a strong corporate culture. This is a subject in itself and will be dealt with in a later chapter.

SUMMARY

❑ All organizations involve ways of breaking down overall tasks into smaller elements and then tying them together again.

❑ This tying together involves two related process:

— co-ordination of specific activities

— integration at the emotional and attitudinal level.

❑ Co-ordination can be achieved in the following ways:

— through line management

— through staff specialists

— through grouping together interdependent activities

— through teambuilding activities

— by means of a matrix structure.

It is unlikely that committees can be effective in achieving co-ordination.

❑ Co-ordination at corporate level involves difficult organizational problems, as size and diversity increase and operations become more complex. Companies can be structured by function, by product, by market segment or by geographical area.

❑ Integration is the process of binding together the various parts of the organization into a cohesive whole. It can be achieved by such means as abolishing boundaries or distinctions between groups of employees, by mobility of personnel, by social interaction, through training and by building a strong corporate culture.

References

1. Katzenbach, J R and Smith, D K (1993) *The Wisdom of Teams*, Harvard Business School Press, Cambridge, MA.

2. Belbin, R M (1981) *Management Teams,* Heinemann, London.

3. Hastings, C, Bixby, P and Chaudry-Lawton, R (1986) *Super Teams*, Gower, Aldershot.

4. Knight, K (1977) *Matrix Organization*, Tavistock, London.

5. Daniels, J, Pitts, R A and Tretter, J M 'Organizing for Dual Strategies of Product Diversity and International Expansion' *Stategic Management Journal*, Vol 6, 1985.

6. Egelhoff, W G, 'Strategy and Structure in Multinational Corporations: An Information-Processing Approach, *Administrative Science Quarterly*, Vol 27, 1982.

7. Bartlett, C and Ghoshal, S (1989) *Managing Across Borders,* Hutchinson, London.

7
MANAGING ORGANIZATIONAL CHANGE

INTRODUCTION

Alvin Toffler[1] tells how in 1968 he received a telephone call from the corporate headquarters of AT&T. A vice-president of the company invited him to spend several years studying the entire organization, offering free access to every executive from the top down on a non-attributable basis, and to address two questions: given the revolution in telecommunications that was now beginning, what should AT&T's mission be, and how should it reorganize itself to carry it out?

Toffler spent four years on the assignment and in 1972 submitted ten bound copies of his report, entitled 'Social Dynamics of the Bell System'. It called for very radical organizational change.

Toffler waited in vain for an invitation to meet the board and discuss his report. The invitation never came. Although there was no official top management reaction to the document it did not simply gather dust on the shelves, nor was it consigned to the incinerator. Photocopies began to circulate unofficially through the management structure and it began to influence people's thinking.

Three years later Toffler met the new chairman of AT&T at a business dinner and was told that the 'underground' report had broken through to the surface and had officially been distributed widely in the organization as a means of stimulating a debate about its future strategy.

AT&T provides an excellent example of a need for organizational transformation arising from changes in market conditions.

Up until 1954, AT&T telephones were standard black. That year they introduced eight colour choices in a standard telephone, and such new products as the 'Speakerphone', the wall telephone, and the 'Princess' phone. This growing diversity of domestic appliances was matched in the business sector with a range of increasingly complex internal communications systems. In the late 1950s the company moved into data transmission services and by the early 1970s was producing approximately 250,000 different service offerings, ranging from small optional add-ons to a customized corporate communications system such as the one installed at Lockheed for a rental contract of $12 million annually. By this time they were producing 1500 different types of telephone.

To create and assemble these increasingly diverse components and products involved a shift from very long to relatively short production runs. Increasingly the sub-assemblies being built into communications systems needed to be individually designed and 'crafted', rather than mass produced. The concept of shorter runs, less routine, more exceptions applied in non-manufacturing areas also. All this increased variety and flexibility created a 'choking sense of complexity'.

These changes in the level of uncertainty generated by new market conditions inevitably meant that AT&T managers and other employees could no longer rely on pre-existing routines or standard procedures as frequently or as safely as in the past. Increasingly, individuals were faced with situations in which they had to invent a new response.

Just as the factory was invented to pump out standardized products, so the bureaucracy was invented to pump out standardized decisions. Bureaucratic systems of organization can perform a limited range of repetitive functions in a relatively predictable environment. Given greater diversity, variety and uncertainty in task and environment, bureaucracy must be replaced by less formal, more flexible structures – by what Toffler calls 'ad-hocracy'.

Toffler proposed for AT&T a highly flexible structure made up of a 'framework' and 'modules', conceived as at the centre of a shifting 'constellation' of related companies, agencies and other external bodies. The framework was described as 'thin co-ordinating wiring'. He believed this loose structural form would overcome three common problems in large organizations – organizational mismatch, over-reliance on top-down decision-making and overmanning – 'just plain flab'.

TWO TYPES OF ORGANIZATIONAL CHANGE

The AT&T case serves to emphasize an important distinction between two types of organizational change.

The first kind can be described as 'reorganizing', or incremental change. It becomes necessary from time to time in all organizations if they are to adapt to changing circumstances. It can be occasioned by simple growth, by diversification involving new products and new markets, by the introduction of new technology, by the need to respond to new sources of competition or to grasp new business opportunities afforded by deregulation. It may simply be the result of a feeling that it is time to shuffle the pack. Incremental change can involve a wide range of decisions and actions – redefining people's roles, creating new ones, regrouping activities, changing reporting relationships, introducing new systems and procedures, modifying or abandoning existing ones. Ideally, following such changes, things improve – such things as higher productivity, improved customer service, growth in market share, successful penetration of new markets and so on. These improvements, however, are often short-lived.

The objective of incremental change is limited. The aim is to adapt or modify an existing social institution so as to make it more effective in achieving its goals, but not to alter its fundamental characteristics. For example, if the organization possesses certain characteristics which, taken together, could justify describing it as a bureaucracy, the purpose of reorganizing is to make it a more efficient kind of bureaucracy, not to transform it into something quite different.

The second kind of organizational change has been described as 'organizational *transformation*', or *radical* change. Here the purpose is clearly to transform the organization into a radically different form of social institution from that which previously existed. Although many of the same actions and decisions affecting structure and systems will be called for as in the case of reorganization – changes in roles, groupings, relationships – they will tend to be more fundamental and far-reaching in nature. In particular, organizational transformation will always involve bringing about changes in values, attitudes and beliefs – the elements of corporate culture. Failure to bring about cultural change will doom to failure any attempt to achieve transformational change.

RECOGNIZING THE NEED – THE 'TRIGGERS FOR CHANGE'

The most commonly recognized signal of a need for radical change is an acute crisis. In the case of the Rover Group, poor financial performance was compounded by a reputation for poor quality, chronic industrial relations problems and intensifying competition, particularly from Japan. Initially it was believed that improvements in communications, suggestion schemes, recruitment and training would be enough to turn the company around. The error in this thinking was subsequently realized and one valuable item in this early programme – an employee attitude survey conducted in 1986 – showed that the whole company system of procedures, practices and management style need to change. Thus the Rover Total Quality Improvement Programme was launched in 1987. Its success in transforming the performance of Rover through gaining the commitment of the workforce is described in Chapter 5.

In Brent Borough Council, the 'trigger for change' in 1988 was a financial crisis resulting in 1000 job cuts out of a total payroll of 7000.

It requires great vision and courage to see the need for organizational transformation and to try to bring it about in advance of a serious crisis, financial or otherwise. Such vision and courage were shown by BP's Bob Horton, on becoming chief executive in 1989. BP was not then in serious trouble – indeed, the climate was one of considerable complacency. Horton's proposed changes were designed to bring about 'nothing less than a change in our culture'. Many failed to see the need for such a radical change, and he encountered considerable scepticism and resistance. Nevertheless it is now widely accepted, both within the company and outside, that the changes he was able to make before his resignation in 1992 have enabled BP to weather the severe economic downturn more successfully than would otherwise have been the case.

BP's Change Objectives

From	*To*
A hierarchical organization characterized by secrecy and status.	A new, flatter organization using openness and recognition.
Bureaucratic organization using formal procedures to control.	Networking organization using values and flexibility to empower.
Multinational organization – comprehensive, highly integrated, obsessed with growth.	International organization: core activities; outsourced functions.
Competitive, individualistic and fast track vertical development.	Co-operative, team focus and horizontal/diagonal development.
Life-time career with high job security.	Continuous change related to known competencies and business needs, with ongoing dialogue on employment.
Low trust management – control.	High trust management – empowerment.

In 'Making it Happen',[2] his account of his successful chairmanship of ICI, John Harvey Jones argues that while it is true that it is very difficult to lead change 'against the grain' of the feelings of the people in a business, it is dangerous to wait until a situation has become sufficiently serious as to build up a powerful head of steam in favour of change. In his view, the art of leadership is to judge the pace of change in people's attitudes and to instigate change before everyone is so frustrated and dissatisfied that they are 'boiling for revolution'.

The dissatisfactions that provide the leverage for change arise when people realize that their livelihoods are threatened by the superior performance of other nations, other companies or other individuals. Harvey Jones points out wisely that such dissatisfaction with the status quo can only develop in conditions of openness and the full disclosure of information. People who work for organizations like ICI where the account books are open and where every employee knows how well or how badly the company is doing are much quicker, in his view, to recognize the need for change than people in organizations which keep them in the dark on such matters.

An approach used by ICI to create a climate receptive to the idea of change has been to send teams of shop stewards and managers to see the competition for themselves and by visiting plants in Japan, Germany and the United States to truly understand, for perhaps the first time, the strength of the competition facing the company. Harvey Jones expresses the problem well when he says that the job of leadership is to persuade people that sticking with the status quo is actually more dangerous than launching into the unknown.

THE GROWING RECOGNITION OF 'PEOPLE' FACTORS IN PERFORMANCE

One thing above all else has led to the focusing of attention on radical organizational change as the means of achieving world-class standards of competitiveness – the growing acceptance of the belief that it is clearly with people that the competitive edge will be found in the case of most industries. We now understand that the really successful businesses of the 1990s will be those which can attract, retain and motivate employees to use their full talents in the interests of the firm.

Siddall, Willey and Tavares[3] point out that in the oil industry the strategies adopted to date have been largely similar, but 'there is little doubt that the growing intensity of competition will signal a change of mood over the next few years'. They believe that the economic drivers and the formulae for approaching external markets are well understood by the major players and that diversity in strategy will be more likely in future to take the form of differences in organization structure and culture.

In the Rover Group, for example, it has become accepted that, in an industry replete with highly competent fast followers, reliance on product features can provide only a short-term advantage. Over the longer run the competitive position of the company depends on its reputation for quality, both in product and service, and on its flexibility and willingness to learn and adapt quickly. These factors are to be achieved by building commitment to delivering extraordinary customer satisfaction and total quality via personal development, line manager leadership and the involvement and recognition of individual employees. Yet just a decade or so ago the conventional wisdom in this business was that the route to survival lay primarily through increased automation, product rationalization and taking a tough line with the unions!

This change in priorities, reflected in many other businesses large and small, has resulted in a new, more strategic role for the personnel function – increasingly referred to as human resource management (HRM). Rover's personnel function has its own mission statement: 'to achieve success through people... and to gain success for the business through the success of its people'. This has guided the work of the function in building the commitment of the workforce, as described in Chapter 5.

The mission involves several elements:

❑ Achieving a profitable partnership with employees through the development of an open environment which provides for an improved quality of working life.

❑ Helping develop and support the leaders which the company needs and hence to help the leaders lead.

❑ Resourcing the company with the right people – right in all respects in terms of numbers, skill and place.

❑ Creating an environment of continuous learning and providing development opportunities for everybody.

❏ Maintaining a continuous dialogue with employees through consistent communication.

❏ Changing how people feel about coming to work by empowering them with commitment, motivation, flexibility and skills to achieve success and fulfilment and so to ensure the success of the individual, the team and the company.

Objectives of this kind are the goals of organizational change today. Rover's results since they were adopted and implemented speak for themselves. The one-time lame duck of the British automotive industry is making good at last – albeit that its future now lies as part of the BMW Group.

TYPICAL ORGANIZATIONAL CHANGE OBJECTIVES AND STRATEGIES

The most common organizational change objective in the UK in recent years has been to achieve radical improvement in standards of quality of product and customer service.
    Other objectives include:

❏ Achieving a more competitive cost base.

❏ Building greater flexibility or capacity for innovation.

❏ Adjusting to market pressures subsequent to privatization or moving to trust status in the National Health Service.

❏ Reorganization following a major acquisition.

❏ Continuous improvement – the creation of a 'learning organization'.

As we have seen in Chapter 1, the actual changes which take place can be grouped under the headings of structural change, adoption of new systems and procedures, and cultural change.

Structural Changes

These include:

❏ Flatter structures – removing layers of management.

❏ The creation of highly autonomous, multi-skilled work teams.

❏ The introduction of more project-based work groups.

❏ Changes in the role of the first line manager or supervisor.

❏ Greater delegation – pushing decision-making closer to the shop-floor or the customer interface. (Often referred to as 'empowering'.)

❏ Introduction of quality circles.

❏ Smaller organizational units.

❏ Breaking down functional barriers, creating internal profit centres.

Changes in Systems and Procedures

Among the most common are the following:

❏ Seeking BS 5750 or ISO 9000 accreditation for the achievement of quality standards.

❏ Just-in-time inventory control.

❏ Statistical quality control.

❏ Single-status personnel policies and practices.

❏ Flexible, performance-related payments systems.

❏ Employee share ownership schemes.

❏ Regular employee attitude surveys.

❏ Continuous monitoring of customer satisfaction and service levels.

Cultural Change Programmes

❏ Development of vision and mission statements.

❑   Training focused on changing values and attitudes, eg achieving a commitment to total quality.

❑   Team building processes.

❑   Relaunching corporate identity.

Some Issues Involved in Changing Organizational Culture

To change the corporate culture involves persuading people to abandon their existing beliefs and values, and the behaviours that stem from them, and to adopt new ones.

The first difficulty that arises in practice is to identify the principal characteristics of the existing culture. In most organizations which have been in existence over more than one or two decades a culture will have developed in an unplanned, unconscious way, as a consequence of the interaction of a whole series of factors.

In the United Kingdom, for example, the culture of organizations will be influenced, *inter alia*, by the following:

1. The geographical roots of the corporation – in the City of London – the industrial North of England – the Scottish lowlands, the Welsh mining valleys, etc.

2. The sources of recruitment of elites. Does the organization have a tradition of graduate entry or, as in the case of the police, is there a tradition of promotion from the ranks? Do the top people tend to be recruited from a particular social class, or from the services?

3. The nature of the organization's basic activity. Is the work dangerous or dirty? Does it call for brain or brawn? Can women do it as well as or better than men? Is it intellectually demanding? Is it highly creative?

4. What have been the business conditions during the organization's formative years? Fierce competition or cosy monopoly? Exposure to market forces or cocooning within the public sector? Operating in stable markets or in ones subject to sharp fluctuations in demand and fashion?

5. What has been the organization's record of achievement? Can it look back on a great and glorious past? Has it been growing or contracting?

Many large organizations which came into being in the early years of the twentieth century in Britain grew up in conditions which have left permanent traces in their cultures. These conditions included:

1. A particularly rigid social class structure in the community, characterized by a considerable status gap between those who, however skilled, worked principally with their hands (blue collar workers) and those who, even at the low skill level of the clerical worker, worked with their brains (white collar workers).

2. A highly protected home market, supplemented by Commonwealth preference, which made it possible to evade intense competition through a combination of cartels at home and/or protection overseas.

3. A strong tradition of mistrust of professionals and respect for the gifted amateur.

4. Ascription of low status to a career in industry or in the engineering professions relative to careers in other professions (law, medicine), in higher education, the civil service, the City or the Church.

5. A social context in which women were expected to concentrate their lives and energies on the home. Their occupational roles were almost exclusively confined to being secretaries, nurses, shop assistants, mill girls or assembly workers in light industry.

6. A world in which consumers were expected to be (and usually were) relatively easily satisfied and in which to complain about quality or service was regarded as a sign of a bad upbringing. A world in which a chronic inability to satisfy potential demand was intensified by acute shortages in two world wars, breeding a 'take it or leave it' attitude.

The cultural features of many organizations which developed during this period are described below.

1. *Complacency bordering on arrogance*   'We belong to a great and powerful organization with an unbroken record of prosperity and with products that are household names. What could we possibly learn from outside sources?'

2. *Conservatism*   'The methods which have brought us success in the past will stand us in good stead for the future.'

3. *Production orientation*   'Marketing is just another word for selling, and salesmen – commercial travellers – are not gentlemen.'

4. *Concern for status and seniority*   The company car, private reserved parking space, membership of the senior lunch mess, one's own secretary – these were the greatest prizes to be won.

5. *A secretive, closed climate* in which information was seen as a source of power and control, under no circumstances to be widely shared. In such organizations even the most trivial communications passed in sealed envelopes marked 'confidential'.

6. *Tolerance of incompetence*, particularly on the part of 'loyal' long-serving and senior members of the organization. There was little effort to manage performance or to deal with problems such as alcoholism.

7. *Lack of sophistication in human resource management* Shopfloor workers were still thought of as 'hands'. If motivation was considered at all, it was assumed that only financial incentives were likely to be effective. Personnel policies supported the blue collar/white collar status divide. Fluctuations in business conditions were dealt with by laying off hourly-paid workers during periods of slack demand.

8. The steady growth of routine practices and procedures to cover every eventuality led to a tendency to treat the rules as ends in themselves rather than as means to an end. The phrase 'It's more than my job's worth' was heard frequently.

9. Women rarely got on in such organizations: 'Their place is in the home.'

It was the development of stagnant bureaucratic cultures closely resembling the above which contributed to the decline of much of British industry and its loss of international competitiveness during the 1960s and 1970s. These characteristics were particularly strong in the motor vehicle manufacturing sector of industry, in the larger textile and clothing manufacturers, in shipbuilding, and in the large, old-established financial services companies.

Today, in the new climate of global competition, set in a more egalitarian society, and one in which women increasingly enjoy equality of opportunity, in a world in which the customer is king and in the context of a growing recognition of the vital role of industry in the life of the nation, new, more appropriate cultures are being shaped. The old values are being scrapped, and new ones put in place.

This is happening in organizations which have carried out an objective and searching appraisal of their existing culture and found it wanting. In most instances where this has occurred two factors have been present. The first is a real sense of crisis – a genuine and widespread fear that the organization's future survival can no longer be taken for granted. The second is the arrival on the scene of a visionary or transformational leader – a John Harvey Jones, a Colin Marshall, a John Egan, a Lee Iacocca (Chrysler) or a Jack Welch (GE) in the USA – a person with the ability not only to develop a vision of the organization's future but also to communicate it to others and inspire them with it.

The new type of culture that is developing is described in different terms by different observers. Sometimes it is called the 'organic' culture, sometimes the 'task-oriented' culture. The main features of companies which have transformed their cultures include:

1. *Profound respect for the individual*   This is the core value associated with IBM's success over the years. It finds its expression in training and development opportunities, greater job security, single status personnel policies and empowerment.

2. *The customer comes first*   In British Airways the core value – putting people first – applies both to customers and to staff. In Marks and Spencer – arguably the world's most consistently successful retail operation – the customer has always come first.

3. *Building teams, creating networks*   Doing things through task forces, project groups and informal co-operation. These things are given greater emphasis. Less and less use is made of traditional hierarchical structures.

4. *Openness and trust*   Sharing information, seeking feedback, using all means of two-way communication to the fullest extent possible.

5. *Delegation, decentralization and autonomy*   Authority and responsibility are increasingly pushed down to the lowest levels possible.

6. *A strong emphasis on innovation*   New ideas are not only welcome, they are actively sought.

7. *Women are treated as persons*   They are judged on their performance and achievements and advanced accordingly.

8. *Dedication to excellence and achievement*   This is all-pervading. Goals are clearly stated. Above-average performance is rewarded and recognized. Advancement reflects ability and performance, not seniority. Poor performers are dealt with in a caring way, but are not left in key positions.

DIRECTING ORGANIZATIONAL TRANSFORMATION

The achievement of lasting culture change calls for a combination of considerable managerial skill and outstanding leadership. We now have enough examples of success and relative failure to be able to draw some useful lessons. The successful achievement of culture change calls for a number of requirements.

Vision

The desired future organization needs to be specified in the form of a 'vision'. To be fully effective, the vision must be clear, easily understood, challenging yet realistic and inspiring.

It helps if it can be expressed pithily in a phrase which is easily remembered – for example, 'The world's favourite airline' (BA), 'A 21st century chemical company – today' (ICI), 'Extraordinary customer satisfaction' (Rover Group), 'Quality, service, cleanliness, value' (McDonald's).

It also helps if the vision is developed in such a way that a wide range of people in the organization contribute to it and thus develop a sense of ownership of it.

In one small organization employing some 300 people it was seen as important to achieve two objectives. First, that the organization's mission should be capable of being expressed concisely in a few words, such that both employees and customers could quickly grasp its essence. Secondly that *all* employees should develop a deeper understanding of the mission and a sense of ownership of it.

It was decided, therefore, to set up a competition in which staff were invited to enter phrases which they felt expressed the core mission. Entries were anonymous and the prize for the winning entry was a flight for two on Concorde. The prize was sufficiently attractive to motivate virtually every employee to participate – and to involve their families, too, in many cases. The motivation of all those who submitted entries was reinforced by presenting them with a Concorde model as a gift for their children or other young relations.

Objectivity

The existing culture must be objectively analyzed and assessed so as to identify those aspects which need to be changed to arrive at the desired future organization.

In carrying out this diagnostic exercise, surveys of employee opinions and attitudes can be supplemented by complementary information from surveys of customers and supplies or the public at large.

At this stage it is often productive to make use of outside consultants whose fresh insight, objectivity and absence of vested interest in the status quo may be helpful in reaching valid conclusions. Ed Schein,[4] in his account of his own experience as a culture change consultant, provides an excellent role model for this type of consultancy. Schein describes how he uncovers what he calls the 'levels of culture'. These are:

1. *Artefacts*   These include all the things one sees, hears and feels when encountering a new group with an unfamiliar culture. Examples are the physical architecture; the language in use; the technology; the products; the organization's style as reflected in clothing, manner of address and displays of emotion; published statements of values; rituals and ceremonies. This heading also covers the visible behaviour of the members of the organization and the organizational processes they have developed. Schein says of the artefacts that they are 'easy to observe and very difficult to decipher'.

2. *Espoused values*   These are the things that people say they believe in, the assumptions that they are conscious of making. Knowing what they are makes it possible to predict what people will say in a given situation, but not necessarily what they will do. Where there are contradictions between the espoused values and actual behaviour, it is necessary to dig deeper and to try to understand the basic underlying assumptions.

3. *Basic assumptions*   These are the beliefs which have come to be so taken for granted that people would regard any alternative way of thinking inconceivable. An example would be the commonly held assumption in the past that anyone in a position of authority in industry would be masculine in gender. Such deeply held assumptions are scarcely ever confronted or debated and are, in consequence, very difficult to change.

Willingness to change

A state of readiness to change must be created. If the organization is in deep crisis such that its very survival is threatened this state of readiness may exist spontaneously. (It is dangerous, however, to assume this is the case. Many British companies in recent years have gone to the wall with their complacency unshaken and their outdated organization practices unaltered).

Implementation

The process of implementing change and doing so in such a way that it sticks is one which calls for intense, persistent and dedicated effort.

The actual business of redrawing organization charts, rewriting job descriptions, drawing up a new incentive scheme or redesigning the performance appraisal forms is a relatively small, albeit vital, part of the process. The greater part lies in bringing about changes in people's actual behaviour and in the values, beliefs and attitudes which underly that behaviour.

The following are some of the most commonly used implementation techniques:

❏ Direct, face-to-face communication involving, where feasible, the entire workforce, but in groups of manageable size at a time so as to facilitate exchange of viewpoints and provide opportunities for feedback.

❏ Role-modelling – here, again, leadership comes in, as top management sets an example by behaving in ways which are consistent with the standards and behaviours that the new organization seeks to reinforce. Such phrases as 'putting customers first' come to life if the top team are seen to be doing so themselves.

❏ Written communications – a whole arsenal of newsletters, posters, stickers, badges etc, all carrying the messages associated with organization change, help to reinforce motivation to change.

❏ Appropriate human resource policies which support the desired changes – these can include:

— revised performance criteria and methods of performance appraisal

— revised remuneration systems

— special schemes for rewarding and recognizing appropriate behaviours.

Investment

There will almost always need to be a very substantial investment in training – not simply to impart new skills, but also to influence attitudes and values.

The programme of organizational change which resulted in the remarkable transformation in performance at British Airways was largely driven by massive investment in training at every level, starting with top management. Thirty at a time of the top 150 people in BA – the policy-makers and those with company-wide concerns – attended a one-week course known as 'Leading the Service Business 1'.

BA directors were among the faculty and the content focused on critical business issues, drawing upon data from staff, customer and competitor research and feedback of participants' profiles on a well-known personality test, the Myers Briggs Type Indicator.

At the next level down there were two three-day residential courses, spaced six weeks apart, for the management teams reporting to the top 150. This programme – 'Leading the Service Business 2' – focused on such issues as:

❑   Who are our external/internal customers and stakeholders and what do they expect of us?

❑   How does our performance compare with our 'functional competitors' in other companies?

❑   How can we contribute to profitability?

❑   How can we exploit IT?

❑   How do we work together as a team?

❑   Do we have the support and commitment of our staff?

Again, the faculty included directors of the corporation, including the chief executive and the finance director. The outcome of each course included a clear mission for each team and plans for securing the involvement of staff in achieving it.

For all employees there was a one-day course entitled 'To Be the Best'. This focused on customer expectations, customer service standards, the competition, the achievement of inter-departmental teamwork and the challenge of seeking continuous improvement.

The course was presented and facilitated by members of BA's middle management and included an opportunity for a dialogue with members of top management. The 'outputs' included suggestions for service improvements, a new focus on customers and competitors, and a greater understanding of the interdependence of the various parts of the organization. The opportunity was also taken to invite staff to express their concerns and to obtain reassurance about the impact of change.

The use of symbolism

John Harvey Jones tells how, on becoming chairman of ICI, he moved board meetings from the imposing boardroom to his own office. The boardroom had been designed in an earlier era so as to emphasize the power of the chairman. Harvey Jones, however, wanted the ICI Board to operate more as a 'band of brothers', with free and uninhibited discussion and with people able to get up, walk around, pour themselves a cup of coffee, draw on flip charts and generally feel relaxed and unrestricted. Under the new arrangement the board members, instead of facing each other across a huge and impressive board table, sat in conference chairs with small, adjustable side tables to take their papers. They sat, more often than not, in shirt sleeves and there were no fixed places. In this way the new chairman symbolized a radical change in management style.

Symbolism of a different kind was used in the transformation of British Airways by the adoption of a new livery. At the time the cost of repainting the whole of the BA fleet gave rise to considerable criticism. With hindsight, however, this symbolic act clearly had its place in a comprehensive programme of change, the pay-off from which more than justified the various investments made *en route*.

The importance of symbolism lies in the way it provides a clear message of a break with the past. Such actions as moving to open plan offices, abolishing reserved parking places, moving to single status catering arrangements or abolishing such traditional job titles as foreman or supervisor can have a disproportionate impact in creating a climate which is receptive to change.

Resistance to change

Top management tend to see organizational change in its strategic context. Rank and file employees are most likely to be aware of its impact on important aspects of their working lives.

Some resistance to change is almost always unavoidable, but its strength can be minimized by careful advance planning, which involves thinking through the factors in the checklist below:

❑ Who will be affected by the proposed changes:

— directly?

— indirectly?

❑ From their point of view, what aspects of their working lives will be affected?

— employment security

— reporting relationships

— earnings

— relations with co-workers

— pension

— other benefits

— career prospects

— status

— workload

— working conditions

— working hours

— skill requirements

— journey to work

— job satisfaction

— training needs.

❑ Who should communicate information about change, when and by what means?

❑ What management style is to be used?

— *Autocratic* Change imposed from above.

— *Persuasive* Attempt to persuade people of the need to go along with changes which top management believes to be necessary.

— *Consultative* Consult employees (through their representatives or directly via an opinion survey) and present a programme of change based on this process of consultation.

— *Fully participative* Only proceed with a programme of change if employees have been fully involved in designing and planning it.

The politics of organizational change

The legitimate power of the board of directors, appointed by the shareholders, is not the sole power base in a complex organization. In the process of directing organization change it is important to be politically astute and to identify potential powerful sources of resistance.

Common sources of power include:

❑ organized labour

❑ the power of expertise, knowledge, or talent

❑ the power of charismatic leadership

❑ the power that comes from exercising control over key resources

❑ the power that resides in the organization's traditional beliefs and values.

Any one, or indeed all of these power sources can be used as the base from which resistance to organizational change is waged. It is a great mistake to believe that such powerful counterforces can be ignored and that the backing of the board of directors will be sufficient in itself to ensure a successful programme of implementing change.

Potential sources of resistance of this kind must be identified in advance and, if possible, their commitment to the proposed changes secured. Where this is not possible a power struggle will inevitably follow – a struggle that the board must win without the kind of compromise that will jeopardize the objectives of the change programme. If necessary, powerful individuals must be moved from the positions of power in the process.

ORGANIZING THE CHANGE

With the foregoing principles in mind, and given top-level awareness of the urgent need for organizational change, it is clear that an action plan is needed, setting out the steps to be taken in sequence, an overall timetable and the allocation of responsibility.

Undoubtedly the most difficult aspect of devising such a plan is deciding where to start, choosing the right kind of intervention which will get things moving. Among the many points of departure which companies have adopted in recent programmes of organizational change, the following are the most common:

❑ Conducting a survey among employees which focuses on the issues facing the business, its strengths and weaknesses and which is so designed as to point to clear priorities for action. The results can then be fed back to employees with the message 'This is your diagnosis of what is wrong with the organization and of what needs to be done – let us work together to take the needed remedial action.'

❑ Carry out a series of presentations as 'roadshows' at which, over time, representatives of top management meet with large numbers of the workforce (ideally with all employees), present their views of the current situation, outline a vision for the future and seek to enthuse the audience to 'buy into' the vision and become motivated to bring it about.

❑ Set up a series of cross-disciplinary or cross-divisional task forces to investigate aspects of the company's operations and report back with recommendations for change.

❑ Pick an issue (the most common ones in recent years have been quality of product or standard of customer service) and focus energy on this using a wide range of tactics such as BS 5750 accreditation, quality circles, customer surveys, etc.

❑ Using a wide basis of consultation across the organization, develop and publish a mission statement.

There are many other possibilities. There is no one way of getting started which will guarantee success. As with so many aspects of decision making at the highest level, it is a question of judgement rather than of seeking for a formula to apply. Much will depend on the degree of urgency involved, the size of the organization, the extent to which the workforce is dispersed over many sites, the extent to which the current organization is one of strong traditions deeply rooted in the past, and the involvement or otherwise of strong trade unions.

How Brent Council Organized Change

Brent Borough Council first committed itself to becoming a customer-focused organization in 1990. In that year it carried out both an employee attitude survey and a customer satisfaction survey as ways of assessing the existing situation. In the same year a vision statement was developed and in 1991 the Council's Total Quality Programme was launched, proclaiming Brent's mission – to be the best local authority in the country. The core values were specified as quality, efficiency and putting the customer first. A fourth – empowering staff – was added later.

At the end of 1991 a senior management development programme was held. This was followed by training 300 'quality facilitators'.

In May 1992 the chief executive held two mass meetings of council employees in the Wembley conference centre to convey the message face-to-face.

It is vital to bear in mind that organizational change is not an intellectual process concerned with the design of ever more complex and elegant organization structures. It is to do with the human side of enterprise and is essentially about changing people's attitudes, feelings and – above all else – their behaviour. Where the organization has a strong and well-developed personnel or human resource management function – one that is represented at board level – the process of managing change will often involve a natural partnership and close working relationship between the chief executive as the leader of change and the personnel or HR director as its leading organizer and facilitator. It is, of course, vital to success that the HR expertise available to the company should be fully exploited. At the same time problems can arise if the programme is seen as being 'owned' by personnel rather than by the line. For this reason it is important that other executive directors in line positions should be allocated clear and responsible roles in the management of the change process and that they are clearly seen to be strongly identified with it.

Some years ago in one of Britain's largest companies a programme of organizational change involved among other aspects a new agreement with shop-floor workers which included the abandonment of certain restrictive practices in return for substantial improvements in pay and conditions, including moves towards single status. The programme was seen very much as 'personnel's baby'. Its official title was 'The Weekly Staff Agreement', but it was known by the initials WSA. Cynical line managers who had not been involved in developing the programme referred to it as 'Work Stops Altogether'. Needless to say it had limited success!

EVALUATING THE CHANGE

It is essential to establish a system for evaluating the extent to which change is actually taking place. This can be done in two ways: first by monitoring shifts in attitudes, beliefs and values. The starting point for many programmes for cultural change is a survey to measure attitudes and beliefs of employees and/or customers. These surveys can be invaluable tools in arriving at an objective diagnosis of pre-existing strengths and weaknesses. Their value is further enhanced if they are repeated at intervals, so as to measure the shifts which have taken place – both the shifts in the values and beliefs of employees, and the perceptions of the behaviour of employees on the part of customers.

A second approach is to evaluate success in terms of results. For example, British Airways set out to achieve, through changing its culture, the goal of becoming 'the world's favourite airline'. It was able to measure and feed back to employees the progress made in approaching this goal by reporting the position in various league tables compiled by the travel industry media. Of even greater significance, however, was BA's rapid emergence as the world's most *profitable* airline.

SUMMARY

The lessons derived from attempts to bring about radical organization change in British industry are now beginning to become clear. They can be summarized as follows:

❑ In most instances radical change – transformation – will be required. Tinkering with the system will get nowhere.

❑ It is difficult to create a climate receptive to change in advance of a serious crisis, but this is what leaders must do. The task calls for both vision and courage.

❑ There has been a growing acceptance of the key role of 'people' factors in achieving a lasting competitive advantage. Hence the main thrust of organizational change programmes is the bringing about of changed attitudes and behaviour on the part of people. This in turn has led to a more strategic role for human resource management.

❑ Organizations are made up of three components: structure, systems and procedures, and culture. Of these, the most difficult area in which to effect real and lasting change is culture. Yet without significant culture change it is unlikely that changes in structure and systems will do much to transform an organization's performance.

❑ The typical objectives of organizational change in recent years have been to improve quality and service, radical cost reduction, improved flexibility and capacity for innovation and a climate of continuous improvement. There now exists a very substantial 'menu' of structural devices, new systems and procedures and ways of producing culture change. Sometimes companies have been unduly influenced by fads and fashion in selecting appropriate strategies. It is very important to be selective and to match strategies carefully to objectives.

❑ The successful achievement of culture change involves many elements, including:

— a clear, widely shared vision and sense of direction

— an objective analysis of the strengths and weaknesses of the existing organization and the identification of needed changes

— the creation of a climate receptive to change

— intense, persistent effort during the implementation process

— a substantial investment in training

— the use of symbolism

— the anticipation and overcoming of resistance to change, including the choice of management style

— understanding the 'politics' of change.

❑ Many things can go wrong. Perhaps the most important pitfalls are, on the one hand, to look for the 'quick fix' and on the other, to expect people to wait indefinitely to see some tangible results from their efforts and sacrifices. It does take a very long time to change corporate culture and to achieve lasting organization change. It is futile to assume that it can be accomplished in one year or even two or three. After seven years of sustained effort in BA, Sir Colin Marshall,[5] in an address to the Royal Society of Arts, said, 'I think that we have started to achieve true culture change'. At the same time enthusiasm and motivation need to be sustained by a sense of achievement over a shorter time-scale. In planning change, therefore, it is important to establish a series of intermediate targets, or 'milestones', at reasonably frequent intervals so that measurable results can be seen to be forthcoming.

❑ The final lesson is that the successful direction of organizational change calls for outstanding qualities of leadership. The managerial competencies of analysis, rational decision-making, planning and scheduling of changes and the like are, of course, both necessary and important, but by themselves they are not sufficient. People will only put their hearts and minds behind major efforts to change things if they are emotionally involved and feel a real sense of mission and purpose. The securing of such commitment and involvement is the leader's unique contribution.

The Role of Leadership

Kotter and Hesketh[6] describe 10 cases of organizational transformation.

In all 10 the major changes began with the appointment of an individual with a track record for leadership. The cases and leaders were:

Bankers' Trust	1977–85	Charlie Sandford
British Airways	1982–5	Lord King/ Colin Marshall
Con Agra	1974–8	Mike Harper
First Chicago	Since 1981	Barry Sullivan
General Electric	Since 1980	Jack Welch
ICI	1982–7	John Harvey Jones
Nissan	Since 1985	Yutaka Kume
SAS	1980–3	Jan Carlzon
TRS/ American Express	1978–83	Lou Gestner
Xerox	1983–9	David Kearns

The leadership process, according to Kotter and Hesketh, involves eight steps, as follows:

1. a leader with a good track record is appointed –
2. one with an outsider's openness to new ideas,
3. who creates a sense of crisis,
4. who creates and communicates a new vision and new strategies,
5. who then behaves accordingly, acting as a role model
6. and thus involves others in key jobs in the drive for change;
7. these others then use thousands of opportunities to influence behaviour throughout the organization,
8. producing tangible results within two years, thus reinforcing the drive to persevere with the change programme.

References

1. Toffler, A (1985) *The Adaptive Corporation*, Gower, Aldershot.

2. Jones, J H (1989) *Making it Happen,* Fontana/Collins, London.

3. Sidall, P, Willey, K and Tavares, J, 'Building a Transnational Organization for BP Oil', *Long Range Planning*, Vol 25, No 1, 1992.

4. Schein, E (1992) *Organizational Culture and Leadership* (second edition), Jossey Bass, San Francisco.

5. Marshall, C, 'Culture Change: No Science But Considerable Art', *RSA Journal*, January 1991.

6. Kotter, J P and Hesketh J C (1992) *Corporate Culture and Performance*, The Free Press, New York.

8
RECENT DEVELOPMENTS IN ORGANIZATION DESIGN

New forms of organization are now emerging and being experimented with in response to the challenges posed by important underlying trends in the environment of business. These include:

- The impact of information technology.

- Increased turbulence combined with intensifying competition.

- Increased complexity as the range of products offered and markets served continues to grow and organizations become more independent.

- The emergence of new sets of values to do with such issues as the quality of working life and environmental conservation.

In Britain the Royal Society of Arts[1] has initiated an enquiry into the nature of 'Tomorrow's Company'. Sponsored by major UK enterprises, including IBM (UK), National Westminster Bank and THORN EMI, the enquiry began by bringing together 25 of the top businesses in the UK under the leadership of Sir Anthony Cleaver, Chairman of IBM (UK). The objective was to develop a shared vision of tomorrow's

company. The interim report of the study, published early in
1994, challenges business leaders to change their approach.
It focuses attention on the central issue – how to attain sustainable business success in the face of continuing and substantial changes in the nature and intensity of global
competition. The report calls for companies to adopt an
'inclusive' approach, ie one that recognizes and seeks to balance the interests of all the 'stakeholders' – customers, suppliers, employees, investors and the community'. It is
acknowledged that this is by no means a new idea but, the
report asserts, for many companies there is a disappointing
gap between words and action.

This particular initiative represents one of the most recent
attempts to find a new model for the business organization –
one better suited to the rapidly approaching twenty-first century than those which have served society since the days of
the industrial revolution.

COPING WITH THE CHALLENGE OF THE INFORMATION EXPLOSION AND NEW TECHNOLOGY

Writing in the *Harvard Business Review*, Peter Drucker[2]
argues that the typical large business 20 years from now will
have fewer than half the levels of management of its counter-
part today and no more than a third of its managers. In its
structure it will bear little resemblance to the typical manufacturing company of the past. It is far more likely to resem-
ble organizations managers pay little attention to, such as
universities, hospitals or symphony orchestras. The typical
business will be knowledge-intensive, composed mainly of
specialists who conduct their affairs by means of a constant
networked flow of information with their colleagues, their
customers and top management. Drucker calls it the information-based organization.

Although many forces are acting together to compel organizations to change, Drucker believes the development of
information technology is the most powerful factor at work.
In his view the organization of the future is rapidly becoming
reality. In *The Frontiers of Management*[3] he cites as examples

in the USA Citibank, Massey-Ferguson and the Erie, Pennsylvania locomotive plant of General Electric. He makes the pertinent point that the organization chart of the information-based system can look perfectly conventional. It behaves quite differently, however, and requires different behaviour from its members.

Information-based organizations are flat, with far fewer levels of management than more traditional organizations. Drucker quotes one large multinational manufacturing organization which cut seven out of twelve levels of management. These management layers were not there to exercise authority, make decisions or supervise operations – their principal function was to act as 'relays' for information, rather like boosters on a telephone cable, to collect, amplify, sort and disseminate information. Modern information technology does a better job. Future information technology will do an even better one still – faster, more economic, and more user-friendly. George Huber[4] paints a picture of voice-operable communications and information processing technologies capable of coaching their users, making available to the organization's decision-makers much more information than was previously available to them. The managers that are left will do things (such as take decisions), rather than co-ordinate the activities of others.

A new principle, the span of communication, will take the place of the old span of control. The number of people reporting to an executive will be limited only by the subordinates' willingness to take responsibility for their own communications and relationships. Control is a function of access to accurate and timely information.

Although information-based organizations need fewer managers, they tend to need more specialists. These people may lack formal authority or hierarchical 'clout', they don't occupy positions in any chain of command, yet they exercise strong influence on decisions and operations, often taking control at times of crisis.

RESPONSES TO THE CHALLENGE OF TURBULENCE AND INTENSIFIED COMPETITION

Faced with the twin challenges of an increasingly turbulent business environment and intensified global competition, organizations are being redesigned so as to achieve ever greater flexibility. John Atkinson[5] points to three kinds of flexibility that are important.

The first is functional flexibility – the ability to redeploy employees rapidly and smoothly between tasks and activities as the nature and mix of the firm's activities change. This can involve moving multi-skilled craftsmen between electrical, mechanical and other technological systems; moving operatives onto maintenance tasks; redeploying administrative personnel into customer service and marketing functions, as happened recently on a large scale in IBM, and retraining people to exercise radically different skills. Thus as changes occur in products, product mix, technologies and processes, the same labour force, more or less, adapts so as to be able to cope, not just in the short term but over extended periods of time.

The second form of flexibility is numerical, the ability to expand or contract the headcount at short notice but without incurring the financial and social costs associated with lay-offs and redundancies. The ideal is to achieve a perfect match at any one time between the numbers of people available to the organization and the numbers needed. The answer lies in a new model of organization in which the traditional view of employment is abandoned and radically different employment policies can be pursued in respect of different aspects of the organization's activities and different categories of worker.

Permanent and stable employment will be restricted to a relatively small number of people exercising core business skills and engaged in whatever has been identified as the organization's primary task. This core group will be expected to display a degree of functional flexibility so as to adapt to changing business conditions, but basically their ongoing tasks will involve a high degree of continuity. These are the key workers – managers, scientists, designers, technicians or marketing and sales staff.

Clustered around them as shown in Fig. 8.1, are various other groups of workers with varying degrees of attachment to the organization – 'loosely coupled' is the currently fashionable term. Some of these occupy the same premises as the core group and are indistinguishable from them – not only to visitors but often to other members of the organization. They include part-time, temporary and casual workers (including in most cases a high proportion of female employees, for whom such arrangements are often ideal) who may be engaged in operational roles such as packing and assembly, or supporting tasks such as administrative and secretarial work or catering. They also include self-employed subcontractors, often engaged in maintenance tasks or in specialist activities such as copywriting, software development or graphic design. On-site subcontractors are used to run whole departments – travel, catering, data processing, printing and security are obvious examples. There will also be temporary workers assigned by agencies.

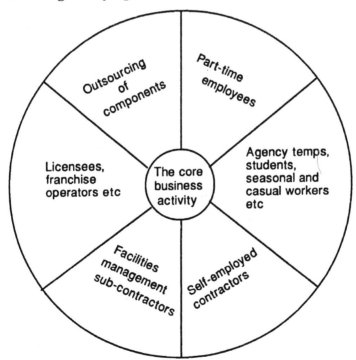

Figure 8.1 *The flexible organization*

The third form of flexibility is financial – the ability to adjust wage and salary costs rapidly (downwards as well as upwards) so as to respond to changes in market conditions, including competitive pressure on costs, shortages of key skills and local labour market characteristics. Financial flexibility is achieved in various ways, depending on the structure of the firm, the degree of unionization and the balance between core and peripheral employees. Local plant bargaining makes an important contribution in unionized companies. The key to success lies mainly, however, in approaches which make it possible to adjust wage and salary costs rapidly in relation to the success or otherwise of the business. Thus performance- or profit-related payment schemes are preferable to ones based on the rate for the job. Where performance-related pay forms a significant part of total remuneration, flexibility is built in, particularly when the bonus pool is related to company profitability.

THE RESPONSE TO GLOBAL COMPLEXITY AND INCREASING INTERDEPENDENCE

Rosabeth Moss Kanter, in *When Giants Learn to Dance,*[6] describes three ways in which organizations are adding to their ability to compete without adding to their existing resources. These are pooling resources with others, allying with others to exploit opportunities, or linking systems in a partnership.

The extent and range of such activity has grown rapidly in recent years, to the point where it has become a central feature in the strategy of some companies. Kanter cites Ford, General Electric and IBM as examples of this trend.

Kanter points to a major change that has taken place in thinking about organization. The traditional view was that the organization existed inside a clearly defined boundary. Other organizations outside the boundary, other than customers and suppliers, were actual or potential adversaries. Increasingly, today, the 'boundary fence' attitude is being replaced by a different concept of organization – the edges are fuzzy and, rather like a Velcro fastener, armed with hooks which can link to other organizations for mutual advantage. Scanning the environment is as much to do with searching for collaborators and partners as with snuffing out the competition.

In the case of Ford, a Harvard professor traced over 40 coalitions between the company and other industrial or commercial organizations. In 1986 General Electric had more than 100 co-operative ventures with other firms.

In some instances organizations join forces so as to provide common services for member firms in a consortium. By 1985 there were at least 40 consortia for research and development in the United States. Among the most important is the Semiconductor Research Corporation, with 33 member firms, including AT&T, General Motors, IBM and DuPont, which sponsors research at several universities. In Britain a consortium of leading organizations, including Marks and Spencer and IBM (UK), was formed to sponsor joint management development programmes for high flyers.

The relationships between organizations engaged in various forms of strategic alliance are fragile and call for careful management. Kanter quotes Corning Glass as an outstanding example of a company which has mastered the art. In 1987 about 50 per cent of Corning's profits came from over 20 partnerships. These include the Owens-Corning Fiberglass Group, owned jointly with Owens-Illinois; Dow Corning, jointly owned with Dow Chemical; and others with Kodak, Ciba-Geigy and Plessey. From the experience of companies like Corning, Kanter has reached some conclusions about what makes alliances work in the long term. She refers to them as 'the six i's'.

❑ The *importance* attached to the relationship is considerable, therefore adequate resources are allocated to it.

❑ There is agreement that the arrangement is for the long term. Thus there is *involvement.*

❑ The partners are *interdependent,* which keeps power balanced.

❑ The organizations are *integrated,* so that the appropriate points of contact and channels of communication are clear.

❑ Each party is kept fully *informed* about the plans and intentions of the other.

❑ The partnership is *institutionalized* – supported by formal legal arrangements, some shared values and social relationships.

The term 'hybrid organization' is used by Powell[7] in an article in the *California Management Review* to describe similar developments. Charles Handy[8] has used the term 'the federal organization' to describe the same phenomena.

Miles and Snow[9] describe associations of independent organizations, which they call 'dynamic networks'. The characteristics of the dynamic network are as follows:

❑ *Vertical disaggregation*   Business activities such as product design and development, manufacturing, marketing and distribution which 'traditionally' were carried out within a single organization are performed by independent organizations within a network.

❑ *Brokers*   Business groups are assembled by or located through 'brokers'.

❑ *Market mechanisms*   The major functions are held together by market mechanisms, rather than by planning and control mechanisms.

❑ *Full disclosure information systems*   Broad access computerized information systems link participants in the network together in a continuously updated data bank.

For the individual firm, the primary benefit of participation in the network is the opportunity to pursue its particular distinctive competence. A properly balanced network can provide the degree of technical specialization associated with a functional structure, the market responsiveness of a divisional structure and the balanced orientation of a matrix.

Companies which appear to be adopting similar approaches to organization include 3M, Hewlett Packard, Texas Instruments and Exxon.

Daniel J Power[10] has identified six novel forms of organization which represent various responses to complexity:

1. *Hierarchical community structure*   Two hundred or more functionally interdependent organizations will be grouped into a five- or six-level hierarchy in which individual organizations will retain a degree of autonomy. Market mechanisms, information systems and specialists in marketing, finance and planning will provide co-ordination and control. Such a large grouping of organizations will become possible as a consequence of the availability of more sophisticated management information systems and communications networks. Strategic planning would be centralized to ensure a view of mission and strategy. However, the identity and discrete nature of each component organization in the community and in the market place would be maintained. Performance measurement and the rewards system would be linked to the performance of each organizational unit and stock options would be used to encourage the best managers to stay with the community.

   Two US organizations appear to Power to be heading in this direction. They are Allied Signal and Alco Standard. Both are conglomerates built up by acquisition, with the acquired companies usually retaining their identity and to some extent their autonomy. In Alco Standard in particular, many of the component companies were previously family-owned and in many cases family members continue to run their companies within the new structure.

2. *Homogeneous, democratic structure*   Organizations without conventional hierarchies may develop as a consequence of improvements in information technology. Small business owners and professionals could merge their businesses and use new technology to share information and resources. They would be federated organizations with power shared among the owners of the individual firms and decisions reached democratically, perhaps using computer-based voting systems. Central information systems and common software would be used to support collective action on pricing, inventory management

and other decisions. In areas of professional expertise, monitoring of standards and assessment of professional competence would constitute additional functions. Examples include, in the US, the Health Maintenance Organizations (HMOs) developed by groups of independent physicians, with each physician having his or her own private practice but receiving services from the collectively owned HMO. Another US example is the brokerage firm Prudential Bache Securities in which the account executives essentially run their own operations under the corporate administrative umbrella. In the UK the BAT Industries subsidiary Allied Dunbar is similarly structured.

3. *Hierarchical replicated structure*   This involves duplicating and co-ordinating operating divisions, again making use of new developments in information processing and communication technology. These relatively independent operating divisions can then readily be divested, should the need arise. This structure would be designed to deal with diverse environments or to cope with uncertainty. Its most likely application would be in the case of companies setting up essentially similar operations in a number of different countries, or operating in a similar way at several sites in a country undergoing severe economic and/or social disruption. It would be a high-cost solution, since most major systems would have to be reproduced within each company.

    Power quotes as an example ITT's telephone company operations, which faced very difficult environments in several foreign countries. The structural solution was to design each national subsidiary to be almost wholly independent of the parent company and easily separable.

4. *Skeletal multifunction structure*   This is a 'mobile' organization, in two senses. First it is transportable, and secondly it is responsive or flexible. It involves a skeletal management team and moveable or transportable, production or service facilities, which at a cost can be rapidly relocated in response to economic or political threats or opportunities. Such an organization would need innova-

tions in production processes and structures to cope with rapid changes in personnel and availability of skills and communications breakdowns. The skeletal core would need structures and mechanisms similar to those used by an army in the field.

The People Express airline had some of these characteristics. At a cost, but in a short time period, it could move its base of operations or 'hub' from one airport to another.

5. *Related network structure*   These are best described as 'tangled structural webs'. They involve a complex combination of interlocking corporations, structural decentralization, project teams, limited partnerships and other structural devices. They may be formed for a variety of reasons – to encourage innovation, protect investments, or to make things difficult for investigative teams from regulatory institutions. Units of the organization will have overlapping and ambiguous functions, and strategic planning in any systematic sense will be difficult.

Companies which tend to show these organizational characteristics include 'shell' companies with no function other than tax avoidance, multiple-level holding companies and other companies which for various reasons resort to complex legal mechanisms to create an organizational tangle.

6. *Extended, hierarchical structure*   This possibility would involve stretching or extending the upper reaches of the hierarchy, with operating personnel forming a relatively small percentage of all employees. Thus spans of control would be narrow and the number of levels in the hierarchy large. Integrated information systems would hold the whole together. Examples, Power argues, are beginning to emerge in large financial services institutions in which information technology is making it possible to automate much of the work at operational level, while an increasingly technocratic managerial bureaucracy is developing in response to growing complexity and segmentation in financial markets.

THE IMPACT OF CHANGING VALUE SYSTEMS ON ORGANIZATIONS

Howard Perlmutter,[11] Director of the Worldwide Institutions Research Center, writing in *World Futures*, outlined his vision of the organization of the future, which he calls 'the symbiotic enterprise'. It is based on a set of values, as follows:

❑ Efficiency and international competitiveness can be consistent with concern for people as individual human beings.

❑ Concern for wealth creation and profit can be balanced by concern for legitimacy by the exercise of social responsibility.

❑ Small enterprise can exist and indeed flourish in the context of large.

❑ Concern for environment and non-renewable resources can be balanced with selective growth and the discovery of renewable resources.

❑ A wide range of technologies can be created and used within limitations deriving from concern about consequences.

❑ Multi-level participation and entrepreneurial innovation can balance the trend towards centralization and increased bureaucracy.

❑ Self-reliance on the part of individuals and communities or nations can be balanced with co-operation and partnership, without descending to paternalism.

❑ Quantity of life and quality of life can be balanced in a world in which the population is still growing.

❑ Rights and opportunities can be tempered by acceptance of responsibilities.

❑ National and international disorder can be reduced through pragmatic efforts at working together taking the place of ideological confrontation.

The enterprise which reflected such a system of values would, Perlmutter argues, survive the coming challenge to the legitimacy of the traditional industrial enterprise which he believes to be inevitable, given the growing gap between the traditional sets of economic and materialistic values on which enterprises have been based in the past and new concerns for individual integrity, for conservation of resources, for protection of the environment and for the quality of life.

Perlmutter sees as the only possible alternative what he calls the 'anti-industrial' enterprise, based on such values as 'small is beautiful', 'intermediate technology' and the belief that profit is immoral and that co-operation produces greater benefits than competition. In Britain, this alternative is well described and passionately argued for by James Robertson,[12] who calls it the Sane, Humane, Ecological (SHE) organization.

Metanoic Organization

Another view of the future organization, based primarily on the impact of changing values, is that of the 'metanoic' organization. The term'metanoic' derives from a Greek word meaning a fundamental shift of mind; it is used by Kiefer and Senge[13] to describe what they perceive as a unifying principle underlying a range of contemporary organizational innovations: that individuals aligned around an appropriate vision can have an extraordinary impact on the world.

At the heart of the metanoic organization is a deep sense of purpose and a vision of a desired future. The vision will, of course, vary from one organization to another, but the alignment of individuals around that vision is the common factor in all metanoic organizations. The resultant level of teamwork is exemplified by that found in winning sports teams, great orchestras or outstanding theatre companies. This teamwork enables the organization to dispense with many of the traditional structural devices used to achieve control and integration.

A further shared characteristic of metanoic organizations is a consistent focus on organization development, with particular emphasis on organization design. Companies studied by Kiefer and Senge had all implemented important innovations in organization design.

One example of a metanoic organization is the Kollmagen Corporation, a manufacturing enterprise in Connecticut which makes a range of products including circuit boards, periscopes, electro-optical equipment and speciality electric motors. The company has a 'small is beautiful' philosophy and is highly decentralized into divisions, each of which has less than 500 employees/$50 million sales. There are 13 such divisions and the CEOs of each report to a divisional board made up of five or six other divisional CEOs and some corporate officers. The key decisions on capital expenditure, research and development expenditure and senior management appointments remain at divisional level. Corporate staff numbers are kept below 25. All employees in a division share in the profits of that division. Within divisions, product teams also function highly autonomously, typically setting their own prices, determining their own sales goals and managing their own production schedules.

Organizational innovation has not stopped short at division level. At the top of the company a 'partners group' has been formed, comprising the divisional CEOs and the corporate officers. The decision-making process is by consensus, and each partner has veto power over any major issue.

Other US examples of metanoic organizations quoted by Kiefer and Senge include Cray Research, manufacturers of one of the world's most powerful computers, the Dayton-Hudson organization – a large retail operation with its head office in Minneapolis, and Tandem Computer.

European companies that have similar characteristics would certainly include Britain's The Body Shop, and Norsk Data in Scandinavia.

SUMMARY

Taking all four streams of influence together it is possible to build a picture of some of the salient characteristics of organizations in the future, as shown in Table 8.1.

Table 8.1 *The organization of the future*

Forces making for changes	Effects of these forces on:		
	Structure	Systems/procedures	Culture/values
The information explosion and information technology.	Flatter structures. Fewer levels of management. Fewer direct workers. Communications networks.	More flexible, more user-friendly. More rapid transmission of timely information for planning and control.	More like the orchestra than the factory. Knowledge and expertise more highly valued than position in hierarchy.
Increased turbulence, intensified competition.	Inbuilt flexibility through separation of core activities from peripheral ones.	Flexible payments systems. Increasing use of IT to develop 'early warning systems' to detect change. Using IT to win competitive advantage.	Development of strong cultural norms in core, focusing on quality, service, cost effectiveness, etc., surrounded by a range of subcultures.
Complexity and interdependence	Fuzzy boundaries. Complex 'tangled' structural networks. Strategic alliances, joint ventures.	Inter-organizational systems for communication and exchange of information. Growing use of expert systems for problem solving.	Development of 'hybrid cultures'. Balancing of value placed on competition with value placed on collaboration.
New systems of values	Networks replace hierarchy. Influence replaces authority. Autonomous work groups.	Development of systems and procedures for evaluating social and human costs of organization's activities. Single-status terms and conditions of employment.	Key values: Putting people first. Respect for individuals. Quality of life. Balancing wealth creation with social responsibility.

This analysis indicates a more or less convergent process – all four forces are pushing in directions which, if not identical, are at least compatible with each other. The art of organization design in the next decade or so will lie in the ability to balance awareness of all four sets of influences. At present, different sets of experts are falling into the trap of looking at organizational issues too much from the viewpoint of a particular discipline. In consequence information scientists concentrate on adapting organizations to the new possibilities opened up by developments in information technology, economists concentrate on the effects of instability and heightened competition in markets, business strategists concentrate on organizational complexity and how to deal with it, while sociologists and conservationists focus on the influence of changing values and challenges to the legitimacy of large scale organization.

Grasping the complexity of organizations of even modest size, understanding the subtle connections between structures, systems and cultures and between the organizational system as a whole and the forces in its environment which are acting on it is an intellectually demanding task of the highest order. To get things even approximately right so that they work reasonably well is a great achievement. The greatest source of comfort, however, is the knowledge that if you do get things even approximately right, you will generate sufficient energy, creativity and commitment on the part of the members of the organization to more than compensate for any design defects.

References

1. Royal Society of Arts, *Tomorrow's Company. The Role of Business in a Changing World*, Interim Report, February 1994.

2. Drucker, P, 'The Coming of the New Organization', *Harvard Business Review*, Jan–Feb 1988.

3. Drucker, P (1986) *The Frontiers of Management*, Heinemann, London.

4. Huber, G, 'The Nature and Design of Post-Industrial Organizations', *Management Science*, Vol 3 No 8, 1984.

5. Atkinson, J, 'Manpower Strategies for Flexible Organizations', *Personnel Management*, August 1984.

6. Kanter, R M (1989) *When Giants Learn to Dance*, Simon & Schuster, London.

7. Powell, W W, 'Hybrid Organizational Arrangements: New Form or Transitional Development', *California Management Review*, Fall 1987.

8. Handy, C, 'The Organizational Revolution', *Personnel Management*, 1984

9. Miles, R E and Snow, C C, 'Organizations; New Concepts for New Forms', *California Management Review*, Spring 1986.

10. Power, D J (1988) 'Anticipating Organization Structures', in J. Hage (ed.), *Futures of Organizations*, Lexington Books, Lexington, Mass.

11. Perlmutter, H V, 'Building the Symbiotic Social Enterprise; A Social Architecture for the Future', *World Futures*, Vol 19, 1984.

12. Robertson, J (1983) *The Sane Alternative,* privately published.

13. Kiefer, C F and Senge, P M, 'Metanoic Organizations in the Transition to a Sustainable Society', *Technological Forecasting and Social Change*, Vol 22, 1982.

SELECTED BIBLIOGRAPHY

The ideas expressed and summarized in this book have been greatly influenced by the work of many writers on organizations. The following were found to be particularly stimulating.

Bartlett, C A and Ghoshal, S (1989) *Managing Across Borders,* Hutchinson Business Books, London.

Burns, T and Stalker, G M (1961) *The Management of Innovation*, Tavistock, London.

Campbell, A Devine, M and Young, D (1993) *A Sense of Mission*, FT/Pitman, London.

Drucker, P F (1986) *The Frontiers of Management*, Heinemann, London.

Garratt, B (1987) *The Learning Organization*, Fontana Collins, London.

Goold, M and Campbell, A (1987) *Strategies and Styles,* Blackwell, Oxford.

Handy, C (1985) *Understanding Organizations*, Pelican Books, Harmondsworth.

Harrison, R (1987) *Organizational Culture and Quality of Service*, Association for Management Education and Development, London.

Kanter, R M (1989) *When Giants Learn to Dance*, Simon & Schuster, New York.

Morgan, G (1986) *Images of Organization*, Sage, London.

Nystrom, P C and Starbuck, W (eds) (1981) *Handbook of*

Organization Design, Oxford University Press.

Peters, T (1987) *Thriving on Chaos*, Macmillan, Basingstoke.

Senge, P (1990) *The Fifth Discipline*, Doubleday, New York.

Schein, E (1992) *Organizational Culture and Leadership*, Jossey Bass, San Francisco, CA.

Toffler, A (1985) *The Adaptive Corporation*, Gower, Aldershot.

Woodward, J (1965) *Industrial Organization Theory and Practice*, Oxford University Press.

INDEX